D1576089

SUCCESSION TRANSITION

A ROADMAP FOR SEAMLESS TRANSITIONS IN LEADERSHIP

More Praise for *Succession Transition*

"*Succession Transition* offers valuable lessons on sustaining your business, no matter your endeavor. Bill Hermann and Gordon Krater are two of the most important leadership teachers of our time by the model in which they lead their lives and inspire their employees, clients, and suppliers. *Succession Transition* is a groundbreaking, practical guide for leaders who want their companies to be sustained into the next generation. You'd pay at least $25,000 for the professional advice contained in this book if you engaged a professional succession consultant."

— *Troy Waugh, CEO of FiveStar3, L.L.C., and author of* Leading an Accounting Firm

"This book is a good lesson about the power that leaders can truly have on the positive outcomes of their organizations and their people when they focus on doing the right things for the right reasons. Corporate strength and longevity do not need to be sacrificed, and in fact can be enhanced, with a plan which helps staff reach their full potential."

— *Kimberly Horn, President and Chief Executive Officer, Priority Health*

"This book is about a lot more than succession as most accounting firms understand it. It's about building a sustainable firm for the ages, and that includes developing the whole human resource. That's what the book is really about, in my mind, with successful transition at the top being one important factor."

— *Robert Bunting, past managing partner, Moss Adams*

"Two experienced professionals share their thoughts on how a succession transition can be orchestrated seamlessly. An easy read packed with great ideas."

— *Eugene A. Miller, Retired Chairman and Chief Executive Officer, Comerica Incorporated*

"This delightful book captures the essence of one of the truly great accounting and consulting firms in the U.S. Bill Hermann and Gordon Krater are veteran leaders who act and speak from the heart. You will want to take out your highlighter when you read this book. Successful transitions are never easy and they don't just happen. The team at Plante Moran has found the right way to do them."

— *August Aquila, CEO, AQUILA Global Advisors, L.L.C.*

SUCCESSION TRANSITION

A ROADMAP FOR SEAMLESS TRANSITIONS IN LEADERSHIP

*By Bill Hermann, Managing Partner Emeritus
and Gordon Krater, Managing Partner, Plante Moran.
With Sheryl James*

MOMENTUM BOOKS, L.L.C.
ROYAL OAK, MICHIGAN

Published by Momentum Books, L.L.C., a subsidiary of HOUR Media, L.L.C.

117 West Third Street
Royal Oak, Michigan 48067
momentumbooks.com

Printed and bound in the U.S.A.

ISBN-13: 978-1-879094-93-2
ISBN-10: 1-879094-93-2
LCCN: 2011936397

Illustrations by Lillian Noga

Contributors

Beth Bialy

CPA, Partner, Practice Unit Leader,

Plante Moran—Government, Chair Participation Committee

Tom Doescher

CPA, Partner, Practice Unit Leader,

Plante Moran—Manufacturing and Distribution Industry

Kathy Downey

CPA, Office Managing Partner,

Plante Moran—Northwest Chicago

Steve Gravenkemper, Ph.D.

Partner, Practice Unit Leader,

Plante Moran—Human Resource Effectiveness

Frank Moran

Founding Partner, Plante Moran

James Proppe

CPA, Group Managing Partner,

Plante Moran—Industry Initiatives

Kelly Springer

CPA, Partner,

Plante Moran—Service and Manufacturing Industry

Contents

Foreword

By Allan D. Gilmour,
President, Wayne State University, Detroit

Why do some organizations last for decades, or even longer, and others falter and disappear from our memories? Major changes in technology, of course, explain some of this. The best livery stable in Detroit, at the turn of the 20th century, is no longer in business. The buggy whip companies disappeared. Henry Ford allegedly said that if he had asked potential customers what they wanted, they would have replied, "faster horses."

Joseph Schumpeter, with his work on "creative destruction," and Clayton Christiansen, with his work on "disruptive technologies," help give us the intellectual underpinnings for what goes on every day as organizations ebb and flow.

But technological change is not the main reason why some organizations prosper and grow and others fall by the wayside. The more common reason for success or failure is the leadership of the organization. And this is where this short but incisive book by Bill Hermann and Gordon Krater is so important; it lays out in a fashion I have not seen elsewhere how leaders are developed and selected for the top positions in Plante Moran.

Organizations, of course, take many forms, from the great companies of the world with a multitude of shareholders (often, through retirement plan investments, including you and me), to smaller businesses, foundations, health care institutions, colleges and universities, non-government organizations, government entities themselves, and the list goes on. They all have in common, either explicitly or implicitly, a mission—what they are trying to do to take care of customers, patients, students, clients, and so forth. They all, except for solo practitioners or proprietors, have employees or colleagues or staff, whatever they may be called.

This leads to the need for any organization of size to have leadership—to have one or more responsible individuals who will lay out where the organization is going, how it should do its work, how it should attract and retain its customers or clients, and how it should measure the results of its work.

But where do the leaders of the organization come from? We see, on almost a daily basis, reports in the business press and on the business cable TV channels of CEOs coming and going. We read in more specialized publications—ones that cover the work of philanthropy, higher education, health care, and many other areas—of new presidents, executive directors, and CEOs. We learn of new managing directors of professional firms. We also reach the conclusion, if we are not careful, that successful organizations need "rock stars" or some sort of stars to lead them. It would appear at first glance that these top positions are glamorous, exciting jobs being filled by the best and brightest (that is, until we see other reports of top leaders being forced out because they apparently failed to meet the demands of the positions they held).

Hermann and Krater puncture this hullabaloo about leaders and leadership. Instead, they lay out a solid approach to succession transition. To them, the transition to new leaders is the product of the methodical development of talent in the Plante Moran organization. Plante Moran starts with the organization's culture of caring and excellence. They recruit those whom they believe will match the Plante Moran culture. They communicate over and over—and over again—the culture of Plante Moran: what Plante Moran is about, and why. They work to develop the careers of all their people. They understand that some are better for professional-intensive work; others are better suited for leadership-intensive work. They mentor, they push, they pull, they encourage.

Because, in the end, it is Plante Moran's culture of selecting the best available talent and nurturing them over years that will provide the potential leaders for whatever leadership needs may arise. They are not forced to call executive search firms to help find new top management talent, because they have grown their own. They do not set up horse races of the most likely candidates for the managing director position, and then see the "losers" leave the firm for other positions.

Plante Moran has an exceptional record of providing outstanding professional services. What Hermann and Krater have written describes, in management-development terms, how they do this—how they build a high-performance organization to provide these services.

It is the most thorough work I have seen. It ignores the fads of the moment. We who are involved in organizations of all kinds will benefit from their work.

—Allan Gilmour, August 2011

Introduction

*By Bill Hermann, Managing Partner Emeritus
and Gordon Krater, Managing Partner, Plante Moran*

In 2008, Plante Moran completed the transition process from one Managing Partner to the next for the fifth time since 1950. We both were prepared for our roles in this transition—but only because of the process that has been in place at Plante Moran for decades. During our leadership transition, there were no power struggles or controversial hand-picked candidates. The firm's day-to-day operations, client service, and long-term planning continued without interruption.

These almost-textbook examples of succession are not just good luck. Good luck doesn't happen five times over nearly 60 years. They have been, instead, the result of intentional planning and a great deal of time invested in ingredients such as great culture, good recruiting, mentoring, technical training, leadership development, and more.

Succession can make or break organizations, large or small. Too often, disputes, family dynamics, competition between candidates, and just plain failure to plan ahead—way ahead—for succession can doom what should be a natural, even joyful time of transition. The best leaders recognize this. Some may name successors well before they step down—"before the lightning strikes," so to speak. This approach also allows successors some time to adjust to the role. It all depends on your organization and your own personal timetable.

Surveys and statistics show that less than one-third of family businesses successfully transition from the first generation to the second. Second to third generation is far worse—well under 20 percent. Other estimates indicate that among the millions of near-retirement-aged business owners, fewer than 10 percent have formal succession plans. This not only imperils the next generation of leaders who will be running these organizations; it hurts clients, and it can make businesses less attractive to potential buyers in the event of a sale. Left unchecked, poor or unplanned transitions can infect all parts of the organization.

The actual task of selecting a new leader is a familiar one to most organizations. Many may not be able to conduct them as smoothly as we do here at Plante Moran.

We hope we can help you find this kind of smooth succession on the day your firm must transfer ultimate authority from one leader to the next. Together, the two of us have more than 60 years' experience at Plante Moran. We both have witnessed successful transitions. We both have had successes and failures, and have seen success and failure.

But we want to emphasize that what we are sharing here is not just what the two of us have learned, but the larger body of knowledge and experience of everyone at Plante Moran—those we work with today, and those who have built our firm. The practices we describe have served us for many years. They worked just as well in 1970, when we had 119 staff and annual revenue of $2.2 million, as they do today, with 1,600 staff and $300 million in annual revenue.

It is, then, the collective and accumulated wisdom of one of the nation's most successful accounting, tax, and consulting firms that forms the basis for this book. It offers concrete steps. But perhaps more important, it offers a great deal of advice—because there is more to succession planning than formality. It is often the informal, between-the-lines knowledge that makes a difference.

As one Plante Moran axiom goes: "There aren't many rules, but there are a lot of guidelines."

There are enough factors that businesses cannot control. Succession is not one of them. With the right planning, process, and execution, you can ensure your organization will not falter because of failure to pass the baton. This book will guide you through the challenging—and, at times, difficult but always dynamic—path of succession. The goal is to have your company remain crisis-free at these most crucial intersections.

Along the way, we will demonstrate how successful succession results from focusing on serving clients and creating a positive business culture that nurtures good staff. This transition model brings stability so that organizational leaders can focus on customers, communities, and business growth—not internal instability and politics. As the book unfolds, you will see that this recipe takes lots of preparation, so you need to start this process well in advance of the decision point.

We identify six areas of focus that help to ensure healthy organizations and, as a result, successful transitions in leadership:

- Organizational culture
- Communication and recognition
- Leadership selection
- Development
- Experiential learning
- Mentoring

Focusing on these areas will allow your organization to grow and to serve clients and staff today, while helping you shape future leaders and pave the way to future, seamless transitions. This will allow you to celebrate your successions and not suffer through them.

"When I'm talking to new clients who have asked for a proposal, it's a big deal to them when they hear about our culture. They like working with a firm like ours that is well-known and recognized for valuing their people and doing the right thing. They can put some faith in the recognition we've received for being a great place to work."

—Gordon Krater

"A positive organizational culture boils down to: How do you act? How do you interact? How would you like to be treated, and how would you like to treat others? A great culture also gives you freedom to create, to try something new, and to challenge. The ability to try something on your own and to take a risk feeds into an organizational culture."

—Bill Hermann

"The culture of the firm is really what attracted me to it 30 years ago. It was clear to me even then that there was something unique about Plante Moran and the people who worked there. When I graduated, there were eight 'Big 8' firms, and I had the opportunity to speak with all of them. The difference in approach, attitude, and general personality of Plante Moran was obvious from the start."

—Kathy Downey

CHAPTER ONE

Building a Positive Organizational Culture

Whether or not you realize it, your organization has a culture. The strength of that culture depends directly on the attention you give it as you grow your organization. Organizations with positive cultures that value staff and clients thrive. Organizations that don't develop such cultures, or preach values they don't practice, can suffer consequences such as poor client service, high turnover, poor staff performance, or stunted growth.

How do *we* define culture? We have a wealth of internal documents, stories, icons, and practices that combine to create the Plante Moran culture. Any staff person can recite Frank Moran's Mayo Clinic model *(see Chapter Two)* or describe work-life balance as being "on the tightrope."

But culture is also the small things: Making sure that we say "hello" to one another in the morning; holding a door open for someone. One well-known story is about a partner who wasn't too busy to stop and help a staff person dig her car out of our Southfield, Michigan, parking lot during a snowstorm.

Culture is easier to recognize than to define. One icon that we use frequently is our "Wheel of Progress" that was developed by our founding fathers. The Wheel of Progress demonstrates a cycle that begins with good staff: *Good staff perform good work. Good work attracts good clients. Good clients are willing to pay good fees. Good fees allow us to pay good wages. Good wages attract good staff.*

This Wheel of Progress demonstrates the powerful connections that create a strong organizational culture. We discuss more about the Wheel of Progress in Chapter Two.

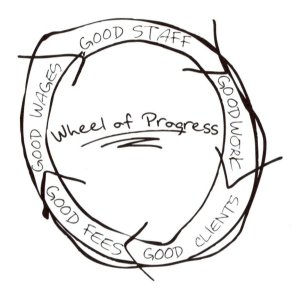

There are also a number of research studies that prove the value of a positive organizational culture. A landmark study by John P. Kotter and James L. Heskett, "Corporate Culture & Performance," examined 207 large U.S. companies in 22 industries over 11 years. The study was the first major academic attempt to examine the link between organizational culture and business profits. It evaluated such cultural qualities as shared values, group behavior norms, managerial behavior, and leadership.

This study found that companies with well-managed cultures increased their revenue 682 percent versus 166 percent over 11 years. Similarly, stock prices increased 901 percent versus 74 percent; and net income increased an astonishing 756 percent versus 1 percent in the poorly managed cultures.

Organizations with strong cultures treat culture as an entity unto itself. It is a shared vision that defines what the organization stands for and how it will function—much like that of a family. At times, certain family members may need extra care. In fact, when talking about mentoring and developing young leaders, we often have drawn comparisons between nurturing organizations and nurturing families.

> **"I think the study of culture is becoming more common, more interesting now.** There are several surveys that measure the relationship between culture and financial performance. I think that gets the attention of leaders. They find out we're not just focusing on culture to feel good, but that firms who have strong cultures and operate effectively seem to do better financially.
>
> "We recently performed a culture survey of a professional services firm. They had had two organizations that merged together and had a strong interest in developing a singular culture. I think in the final analysis, what we believe is that it's not really the parts or the tools that create the culture, it's the culture that creates the tools."
>
> — Steve Gravenkemper

Benefits of a Good Culture

A good culture can help reduce your staff turnover; it can also help you win new clients. In one instance, Plante Moran was working to secure its largest-ever single consulting client. The client took a long time in its selection process because of various internal issues over which Plante Moran had no control. So it was a matter of working hard and then just waiting. Meanwhile, other competitors, one in particular, also were wooing this client. There was no way to tell how close they were to securing the contract.

This waiting and wooing went on for nearly a year. But in the end, the client selected Plante Moran for one major reason: staff consistency. The same team that had begun working with this client was still in place a year later, when the client was ready to decide. The other firm vying for this business had experienced nearly 100 percent turnover.

A strong, positive culture transforms an organization into a kind of family—an environment that is not the reflection of one person, but of all, and is nurtured and cared for by everyone. It is through this shared vision that institutional knowledge is passed, future leaders are groomed, and stability is created and maintained.

Clients are not the only ones who appreciate a good organizational culture. Staff ranks it above most other considerations in the workplace. For instance, a survey of Plante Moran staff revealed that culture is the No. 1 reason they joined the firm—and why they stay here.

A full 70 percent of Plante Moran staff ranked firm culture ahead of growth opportunities, pay, client services, and other reasons for staying. Other surveys find similar results.

A Positive Organizational Culture

"A few years ago, representatives from a large, well-known company in metro Detroit asked if they could visit Plante Moran, and they were candid about why they were coming. They knew Plante Moran had been selected fairly consistently as one of *Fortune* magazine's '100 Best Companies to Work For.' The visiting company never had come close to winning this honor, and they wanted to see what kinds of business practices led to such recognition.

"A group from their Human Resources Department came over and immediately noticed friendliness and caring among all staff, which extended to Plante Moran visitors, too. More than one person stopped to ask if they had been taken care of. I was one of them. I happened to be in the lobby shortly after this group arrived. These visitors did not know I was the Managing Partner when I offered a simple hello and asked if they needed any help. After learning later who I was, one member of this visiting group could not help but share with me his initial observations.

"'You know, we came here to find out why you're on the *Fortune* list every year and we're not,' he said. 'I'm not sure I even need to stay any longer. First, I pull into the parking lot and see a sign on several of the closest parking places that says, "Expectant Mothers." Then, someone holds the door open for me, greeting me and asking, "May I help you?" I walk in the door and notice people are smiling and saying hello to each other. Then the Managing Partner of the firm walks through the door in a very unassuming way and asks if we've been taken care of before he heads to the elevator.

"'I think I know what the difference is. There's a friendliness, a willingness to help others and sense of enjoyment in what everyone is doing.' "

— Bill Hermann

Still, defining "organizational culture" is not easy. Some compare it to nailing Jell-O to the wall. Some think culture is little more than a framed list of company policies exhibited in the company reception area.

It's just not that simple. Instead, it's the values and behaviors epitomized by everyone—from the top down. It's how people behave, how they treat one another inside and outside of the firm. It is more than processes and procedures, though processes and procedures do provide structure—especially as companies grow.

Plante Moran's reputation as a culture-driven organization goes back to co-founder Frank Moran, an accountant and philosopher. Moran pioneered many of the philosophies that guide us today. The generations since Moran have helped to interpret and expand on his philosophies. You might say these successive generations have accepted the seeds he planted and have facilitated growth ever since. Frank Moran provided the platform; the rest of us must continue to maintain it.

In addition, it's important to remember that good organizational cultures are proactively built; they don't just fall into place with good intentions. It takes time to define, communicate, demonstrate, and reinforce your culture.

Once established, good cultures also need to be maintained and refreshed—especially as companies grow from a handful of people to hundreds or even thousands. New ideas enhance culture. Such ideas can come from company mergers, new challenges and even enterprising new staff members. For example, as the percentage of women increased in the ranks at Plante Moran, the issue of child care became more apparent. This led to the introduction of Saturday daycare services during the busy tax season. While the advent of more women in the firm initially brought the issue to light, the daycare services quickly benefited all of us.

In fact, it's interesting that the establishment of the Saturday daycare had some unintended complexities. Beth Bialy helped administer that program early in its inception, and there was some worry that it might conflict with the positive culture. She said there was fear establishing this service would be translated as, "Hey, we're making daycare available, so you better get in here and work." Saturday work was never mandated, she says. The daycare was just a courtesy for those who chose to come into the office those days.

Ironically, as technology has allowed staff to work from home, more and more Saturday daycare users are male staff giving their wives a day to catch up.

Failure to establish a good culture is one of the most difficult things to fix, so it needs to be in place as soon as possible. Building such a culture begins with some basic principles.

The first step is to identify one overriding and guiding principle. Plante Moran, for example, cites the traditional Golden Rule: "Do unto others as you would have them do unto you." This was first cited by co-founder Frank Moran. The Golden Rule, or a similar guiding principle, can serve as a foundation for your firm's strong organizational culture and workplace.

Providing good client service and building a pool of talented leaders requires a truly world-class culture that helps us retain our top talent. Below are additional steps to a good culture.

IDENTIFY, ARTICULATE, AND *LIVE* YOUR COMPANY'S CORE PURPOSE, VALUES, AND GUIDING PRINCIPLES.

Whether you're working with a startup company or a mature organization, you need to identify and articulate your company's core values and guiding principles. And then, everyone must live them, starting with those at the top. No one gets a "pass." Physical buildings need good foundations; so do good organizational cultures. Everything relating to your culture rests upon your core values and principles.

For example, Plante Moran's core purpose is: "To be a caring, professional firm deeply committed to our clients' success." Developing a similarly centralized, guiding vision will anchor your efforts toward establishing a discernible, positive business culture.

Core values and guiding principles come next. It's important not only to make these clear in formal staff materials, but to reinforce them in more participatory venues. An initial workshop about these principles, during which staff can ask questions and suggest updates and improvements, is effective. Referring to these principles frequently also helps drive home that these are not just empty corporate mantras.

Underlying any list of core values and principles is trust—plain and simple. Knowing and trusting that people you work with care,

are telling you the truth, and will do what's right for the firm—each time, every time—is invaluable. We both realized the primary example of trust when we each took over as Managing Partner. At that point, we realized that we had only one client: Plante Moran.

Other important company values and principles should center on these concepts:

Show your staff you care.

"Caring" is a soft, overused word, but it packs a lot of punch when it's demonstrated in real, discernible ways. It begins with small measures, such as our practice of using the word "staff" instead of "employees." The latter implies that one "works for" the other, a concept that's out-of-sync with the partner-team environment we hope to encourage.

Overall, the goal is to create a challenging yet supportive environment that will allow staff to reach their potential. All of this will help you avoid the results of poor management practices that too often accompany such goals: forced long days at the office; little attention to family concerns; high pressure tactics that emphasize punishment for "failure" and largely ignore rewards for jobs well done.

Some other guidelines:

- **Don't tolerate substandard or crass behavior—from anyone.** A popular saying at Plante Moran is that we are "relatively jerk-free." Why "relatively" jerk-free? Everyone knows what a "jerk" is, and everyone certainly knows when they see one. Everyone also can be a jerk temporarily, without realizing it. So the idea is to hire and groom carefully, which is addressed more in Chapter Three. Behavior that lacks respect, civility, and fairness is not part of a positive business culture. The smaller the firm, the more impact one "jerk" can have.

  What is a "jerk"? An example might help. One of our young managers tried to motivate a new staff member by giving him a denigrating nickname, thinking it would encourage this staff member to work differently.

  This manager received a call less than a half-hour later from one of the firm's management team members, who asked him what in the world he thought he was doing. The manager learned his behavior did not reflect our firm's core values and the Golden Rule. He was reminded to keep his negative feelings to himself, and to find more respectful ways to address staff motivation. Even this coaching, which was the result of less than

---

A Team Environment

Everyone at Plante Moran has an advisory team who participates in their performance reviews. Staff members meet semi-annually with this team; partners meet with their teams annually. This isn't the perfunctory performance review that so many organizations have, but an investment to help individuals grow. While there is a discussion about performance, the lion's share of the conversation is about the future. It forces everyone to think about the talents the individual wants to develop and the experiences they need to reach their potential. It provides insight into strengths that individuals may not recognize they possess, and candor about blind spots. All of this is served with a healthy dose of praise and gratitude.

PLANTE MORAN
100% jerk-free*
*Almost. C'mon, no one's perfect.

desirable behavior, was administered in a caring and supportive way, which allowed the manager to go on to enjoy a long career with the firm.

- **Recognize your staff's work-life balance.** People live a constant balancing act—a tightrope, if you will, between their professional and personal lives. They face daily the necessity for balance between pressures at home and at work. The entire person comes to work, not just the professional. If a staff member has a sick child, struggling teen, or aging parents who need extra care, he or she is naturally less focused at work. Understanding such pressures and making room for them is important. Balance is crucial for staff to remain fully productive and happy.

  Keeping tabs on this work-home tightrope requires some conscious work. Consider establishing a committee to monitor issues that affect work-life balance, and come up with potential solutions. In the past, companies have instituted child care services, expanded leave of absence policies, part-time work opportunities, and other measures to help staff balance their home/work responsibilities. Also, furnishing staff, including administrative staff, with up-to-date technology—such as laptops and networks that allow mobility—gives them even more flexibility in the event of child care, medical, transportation, and other issues.

- **Create a workplace that reflects your core values.** Avoid hiding top-level managers in an executive suite of offices or a special "partner row" set apart from other staff. When top management practices the culture in their day-to-day routines, it is a powerful model for others.

- **Help new hires feel at home.** Starting a new job is bewildering for anyone. New hires often wonder what to say or do in their first weeks and months on the job. Make sure you offer ongoing learning and mentoring—which we detail in subsequent chapters—from the beginning. New staff should not feel "new" much longer than it takes to walk in the door their first day on the job. This can establish loyalty early on and help minimize turnover.

Fairness also anchors a strong business culture.

Treating staff and clients with genuine fairness is something they recognize, no matter what the situation or business transaction. Overall, fairness can resonate in virtually all actions at a company, but it requires constant vigilance.

"We strive to be fair," is one of our core values, and the concept of fairness resides in three overarching principles at Plante Moran. They are filters through which all decisions, big and small, are made. The first is to "optimize versus maximize." This principle is illustrated in such decisions as to have a smaller ratio of partners to staff, which is a different model than what many other firms follow. The result is more client service by partners on engagements rather than less experienced staff.

Doing the Right Thing "I was dealing with a potential new client shortly after I had made partner. We started with a small portion of the client's work and I was asked to try to build a relationship with the client. The client had made it clear that if they were pleased with this initial work, Plante Moran would win the client's entire business.

"New and nervous, it wasn't long before I discovered the client had violated a bank covenant and did not want to disclose it—which clearly violates our professional standards. While the client initially indicated they had a waiver and would produce it, as the filing deadline approached, they never produced one. Finally, they admitted they did not have the waiver, but wanted us to complete our work, ignoring the fact that they had a violation. I returned to the firm and spoke with everyone, including the Managing Partner and the head of professional standards. There was complete unanimity: This was a black or white issue; the client's request was wrong. The head of professional standards told me, 'We could make a lot of money in the short term doing things like this, but we'll go out of business in the long term.' The money didn't matter. We dropped the client, and my loyalty to the firm increased tenfold."

— Gordon Krater

The second principle is "to do the right thing for the right reason"—for example, keeping a commitment to hire graduating seniors even though the economy has weakened since the offer was extended and your needs have been reduced. There are many, many other times when this phrase will guide your overall success for individuals and the firm.

Finally, in a "one-firm firm," all profits go into one pot. All resources are used to serve all clients, regardless of industry, location, or profit center. This concept, identified in a 1985 *Sloan Management Review* article by David Maister, helps establish institutional loyalty and team focus through such practices as highly selective recruitment, heavy emphasis on developing talent rather than going outside for it, discouraging a "star system," pay based on group rather than individual performance, and much more.

In a 2006 article on his website, Maister wrote, "Loyalty in one-firm firms ... is based primarily on a strong culture and clear principles rather than on the personal relations or stature of individual members.... The key relationship is that of the individual member to the organization, in the form of a set of reciprocal, value-based expectations. This, in turn, informs and supports relationships among members—who often do not know each other personally." Maister noted this concept is used especially well by the U.S. Marines, so it is applicable in many groups.

Quality and integrity.
Quality and integrity are valued by your clients and potential clients. Put your clients' needs before your own. Know the rules in your business domain, adhere to them, and exhibit them. Where is the line? What constitutes stepping over the line, and are you scrupulous in avoiding doing so? If you can answer those questions positively, and hire staff that can as well, you will be a leader and a company others seek out for advice.

Be consistent.
Don't change your rules or your behavior guidelines, even in times of crisis—or in times of great profits. The intent of what you say and what you do should remain consistent, even when that can be hard to do. Your company may have several office locations. Each will have its own personality. While you need to allow room for individuality, all should implement the company culture.

Be kind, but be candid.

A Frank Moran saying, "candor is kindness," bears great wisdom. In the midst of a culture that centers on humanity, kindness, sharing and mutual support, telling someone the truth can be challenging. Still, failing to communicate a crucial truth—managers to staff or vice versa—only hurts the person who most needs to hear it. One simple example: One manager was told by a partner that he had coffee breath. Simple, yes, but important, especially in the context of client meetings. That manager, now also a partner, never has forgotten this kind of feedback. Other corrections can make a difference in a person's career, learning, and overall comfort level.

SUMMARY

1. Whether you realize it or not, your organization has a culture.

2. The strength of your culture depends directly on the attention you give it as you grow your business.

3. A major study found that companies with well-managed cultures versus poorly managed ones increased their revenues 682 percent versus 166 percent.

4. Good cultures help reduce staff turnover and help win new clients. Staff generally rank good culture above most other considerations in the workplace.

5. A strong business culture helps support natural, orderly leadership transitions.

6. Culture boils down to the values and behaviors epitomized by everyone in the firm, starting at the top.

7. Good business cultures are proactively built. Here are some steps:
   - Begin with one overriding, guiding principle.
   - Specifically identify your core purpose, values, and guiding principles.
   - Live these core values and principles.

8. Any list of values and guiding principles should revolve around certain basic concepts:
   - Show your staff you care.
   - Don't tolerate substandard or crass behavior—from anyone.
   - Recognize your staff's work-life balance.
   - Create a workplace that reflects your core values.
   - Help new hires feel at home.
   - Instill fairness, quality and integrity, consistency, and kindly delivered candor.

"The way an organization communicates reveals a lot about its culture. The stories, icons, symbols, and even catchphrases that are passed on from one generation to the next can bind people together and create a sense of community."

—Gordon Krater

"As a leader, you need to embrace the theory that there is no such thing as over-communicating."

—Bill Hermann

CHAPTER TWO

Culture and Communication

Culture is spread and preserved by the stories people tell, and that same concept holds true in the workplace. Every organization has its own "lore"—stories that are repeated during formal and informal occasions. These stories connect staff to one another in a fundamental way. They also bring an organization's core beliefs and culture to life.

We tell numerous "stories" at Plante Moran, and one that demonstrates our culture and resonates with the notion of culture and succession planning is the "Mayo Clinic" story. Our co-founder, Frank Moran, often said that our goal was to be like the Mayo Clinic, an organization that instantly evokes undisputed quality. He asked us to envision a building where staff who wanted to work here were lined up on one side, and clients who want to be served lined up on the other side. By evoking a familiar name like the Mayo Clinic, he instantly created a "short cut" to illustrate his vision for the type of firm we should be striving to create.

Effective leaders find ways to tell these stories and to introduce new ones.

If stories are a way to build culture, then nothing kills culture quite like the failure to communicate effectively. Here are some general principles for enhancing your culture by good communication.

ESTABLISH AND MAINTAIN EFFECTIVE COMMUNICATION CHANNELS

People want to hear about their company's vision, obstacles, and plans for the future. If your staff members don't have a clear sense of where you are today, where you're going, and how you'll get there, they can't participate in the journey. It's important to collaborate on your vision. Through communication practices, you can leave no questions unanswered—including ones staff haven't thought to ask.

> **"Plante Moran's Associate Meeting tradition is one example of transparency.** Transparency is evident when the firm's management team members meet annually with the Associates (manager-level staff). I remember the first time I had an Associate Meeting as Managing Partner. I had received questions ahead of time. The first question I received was, 'What are the average partner earnings?' I don't think we ever had discussed it before. I asked the management team what to do. We decided to go ahead and share the information."
>
> —Bill Hermann

A well-defined annual communication calendar can be a valuable asset in this regard. By planning the communication strategy well in advance, key messages can be spaced, minimizing the opportunity for anything to fall through the cracks. A simple message to say thanks for a job well done or happy holidays should hold an important place in your communication calendar as well.

Here are some ways to communicate effectively:

Be as transparent as possible.
Open leadership is effective leadership. Top leaders have a great deal of latitude by their very positions. Their decision-making process

should be shared throughout the organization. Staff will see why certain moves are made and will be able to ask questions or offer input. Such transparency results in high levels of trust by staff.

Roadmap major changes.

Communicating the future direction, or vision, of the firm to the entire organization is senior-level management's primary role. This responsibility is even more important when major changes are necessary. As companies go through growth stages, there will be many instances when communication will play a key role in managing major changes.

Try to communicate changes effectively, broadly, and with as much enthusiasm and optimism as is credible. Since people absorb information differently, leaders should be available for follow-up questions at any time, no appointments necessary. The more informed staff are about a firm's goals, accomplishments, and initiatives, the more they will feel part of the team and want to stay and participate. A "frequently asked questions" document can be a good tool to help address questions as people process the information.

Communicate in lots of ways.

Along with face-to-face meetings, use vehicles such as e-mail, intranets, blogs, and voicemails to share company news. Variety adds to the effectiveness of communication by "mixing it up." You might use these tools to pass along success stories, firm initiatives, updates on the firm's financial standings, new scheduling systems, congratulations for a job well done, or just a simple "happy birthday."

Maintain an open-door policy.

Nothing telegraphs closed communication more than closed doors. Open doors symbolize open lines of communication and can encourage more frequent and open dialogue. Open doors help set the stage for an attitude that conversations are part of everyday business practice. Such questions or conversations don't have to wait for special meetings, company conferences, or annual reviews.

Casual communication conveys camaraderie.

Chat with staff members as you pass by their desks. So many firms' senior level managers are neither seen nor heard from; it's as if they're reluctant to talk to their staff. Some simply may have gotten out of practice of such communication.

Avoid such isolation. In the break room, ask team members how things are going. Personally drop off that birthday card or the holiday present. As near-obsolete as they may seem, nothing resonates as much as a handwritten note or letter. These practices don't always have to be linked to staff successes.

We also conduct regular meetings to keep staff members informed and involved.

The most important is our annual firm conference. This one-day event is held off-site and the entire Plante Moran family attends. At this conference, we share progress, celebrate successes, and rekindle friendships. We encourage a lot of fun and creativity. Our alumni and former staff members share fond memories of this tradition. Many recall conferences that moved or motivated them in new ways.

This event began as a weekend getaway for partners and staff. As the company grew and expanded, it was consolidated to the current, one-day format. It will evolve further as we grow. But we will maintain our original commitment to open dialogue and celebration of success.

We also hold semi-annual partner meetings. We feature breakout sessions and host outside speakers that help us broaden our perspectives. These gatherings emphasize information-sharing, table-group exercises, and opportunities for partners to discuss important issues facing the firm.

Finally, we have a tradition of fall associate meetings where one or two members of our management team meet with the associates in all of our offices. Associates are "non-partners." Most associates have been with the organization at least five years. By definition, the associate groups are full of individuals who will grow into future firm leadership positions. These sessions are usually based on questions submitted by the associates. No topics are off limits, and management team members in the sessions promise "no holds barred" answers. They are a popular Plante Moran tradition, and everyone comes out of these meetings feeling better and more informed.

These formal processes are crucial. But equally important are impromptu events that allow leaders and staff to sprinkle information into ordinary, day-to-day conversations. These contribute greatly to weaving the cultural fabric of the firm. For example, a group of partners and staff have an annual trek to an ethnic restaurant for lunch in Hamtramck, Michigan. On the face of it, this is an annual lunch, but the insights and camaraderie formed and shared are deposits in what you could call the "spirit bank" all year long.

RECOGNIZE AND REWARD GOOD WORK.

Praise over punishment.

Motivating, developing, and mentoring staff is detailed in subsequent chapters. Suffice it to say that when it comes to encouraging good work, praise trumps intimidation or fear every time. Parents know this; managers should, too. Many do not.

One major company, for example, managed through intimidation and fear. In their sales group, forecasts were requested multiple times per day, and intimidation was routinely used when sales budgets were missed—despite the economic realities at the time. People's jobs were routinely threatened before any underlying cause-and-effect was investigated.

Such tactics created nothing but anxiety and deprived management of the information that would help improve future sales. This approach also created a cycle of poor sales and high turnover. The good performers left as soon as possible and the poor performers held on as long as they could survive.

Create instead an environment where staff contributes more because they want to and because they are recognized for good work when it occurs, not only at annual reviews. Just telling a staff member they did a good job goes a long way. Compensation and promotions are effective motivators, as well—as long as they are fairly applied, of course. Finally, everyone makes occasional mistakes. How you respond to these can make a real difference down the road with talented staff members and potential leaders.

Offer some specific awards.

These can be awards such as Staff Member of the Year, or Sales Rep of the Year. At Plante Moran, we offer a "Speak Up" award for the staff member who offers the most constructive suggestions to improve business procedures or processes. Other awards can recognize the work some staff do to promote spirit or those who exhibit the most willingness to help others each year.

Have some fun.

Even small firms can adopt these ideas; having fun doesn't have to cost a lot of money or require travel to swank resorts. Whatever your size, don't limit your fun factor to holiday parties and the obligatory company picnic. Establish some formal and less formal opportunities. Consider spontaneous breaks and humorous moments. Celebrate birthdays, anniversaries, and retirements.

Take advantage of community points of pride. Consider trips to professional ball games, the best golf course in the area, or attending major city celebrations. Be creative. One of Plante Moran's most popular activities in its Detroit-area offices is a Detroit Tigers Opening Day Luncheon. A smorgasbord of ball park goodies such as hot dogs, nachos, ice cream, and White Castle hamburgers are brought in while staff members enjoy watching the game during lunch.

> **"I remember as a young staff member, I helped a client come to the firm.** It wasn't a particularly big or special client, just one of our more typical clients. But the Managing Partner personally walked into my office and thanked me and talked about what I had done. And I thought, 'I'll sure do this again.' We've all had those experiences, but it's taking that extra half-step, even when the firm is large. It's going back to: 'How would I act if I were in a five-person firm?' This kind of communication should transcend size."
>
> —Gordon Krater

All of these steps are important, but how do you maintain a good culture as your organization grows? For instance, as Plante Moran has grown, we have added formalized business processes that were not necessary during our earlier, smaller era. A governance structure and a performance management system had to be instituted. These more formal practices could have undermined the culture that flourished in a cozier, less formal environment.

We offer the following fundamental actions to maintain culture as your firm grows:

- Your top-level managers, or partners, must be committed to maintaining the culture.
- Talk consistently about maintaining the culture by using every opportunity to refer to your core purpose and principles.
- Continue to reinforce the behavior that defines your culture.

Consistent communication and recognition help us fulfill our commitment to clients and staff. They are the foundational steps introduced in Chapter One. Plante Moran, as a professional service firm, has a mandate to serve its clients. That mandate has driven our focus on clients and staff, and consequently our culture. This circular analogy—the link between business culture and good business—is illustrated by the "Wheel of Progress," which dates to the days of co-founder, Frank Moran:

Good staff perform good work. Good work attracts good clients. Good clients are willing to pay good fees. Good fees allow us to pay good wages. Good wages attract good staff.

"Good staff" is a well-trained, supported, and content group of committed individuals who believe in our overall business philosophy.

"Good work" exceeds industry standards. Constant communication and follow-up by staff further enhances the quality of this work.

"Good clients" mean solid organizations, large or small, who want to "do the right thing," in the parlance of our day. Good clients also have leaders who are knowledgeable and effective enough to run their businesses, and mature enough to accept advice.

"Good fees" mean fair fees—not excessive fees. Fair fees are at the heart of client service, so "profits will take care of themselves," as Frank Moran put it. To date, no Plante Moran client complaint that fees did not match services delivered has gone unresolved. One way to put this: Don't generate fees. Generate services.

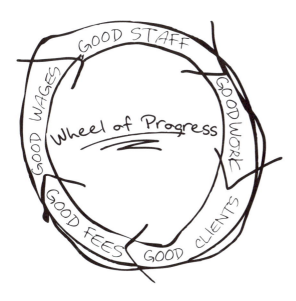

"Good wages" is self-explanatory, and is the last link to our original building block of good staff.

All of these attributes help define an organization's culture. A deep culture communicated consistently by all leaders, regardless of who is at the helm, provides a solid foundation for organizational growth. Too often new leaders use their time in office to "reshape the culture" to their own style, which may explain the reasons some organizations come and go from "best places to work" lists. A solid culture that is broad enough to embrace healthy change, yet structured enough to ward off negative influences, enables organizations to avoid failure during declines—and provides a solid foundation for successful succession and transition from one generation to the next.

The next chapter will focus on the all-important topics of recruiting and re-recruiting staff—what it takes to attract, train, motivate, and retain the best candidates, and help them reach their highest potential.

SUMMARY

1. Communication is a key pillar in a positive culture.
2. Communication rests on transparency and other key practices:
   - Roadmap major changes. Senior management needs to inform all staff of future plans.
   - Communicate in lots of ways—by personal meetings, e-mails, voicemails, blogs, notes.
   - Maintain an open-door policy.
3. Recognize and reward good work. Praise is far more effective than punishment.
4. Offer rewards and awards for staff accomplishments.
5. Have fun. Have formal and informal activities that help relieve stress.
6. Maintaining culture can be difficult as your firm grows. Keep the following points in mind:
   - Your top-level managers, or partners, must be committed to maintain the culture.
   - Talk consistently about maintaining the culture by using every opportunity to refer to your core purpose and principles.
   - Continue to enforce the behavior that defines your culture.

"Hire right, or manage hard."

—Bill Hermann

———✳———

"The last thing you want is for everyone you hire to be like you. Eventually, you just breathe in your own exhaust."

—Gordon Krater

CHAPTER THREE

Leadership: Selection/Projection

Finding future leaders begins with recruiting and hiring. Whether recruiting on college campuses or hiring experienced individuals, you are looking for the next generation of leaders. There is nothing haphazard about recruiting and hiring the right people for your organization. Every step is intentional; this is not a casual or quick process.

Plante Moran has refined its recruiting process over many years. As a result, we can identify recruits who have the "right stuff": interpersonal ability, technical skill, professionalism, and cultural fit.

We believe you can't shortcut the decision to attract the right kind of people. You have to look for those you think will fit into your culture. That doesn't mean we all have to look the same or think the same. Hiring the right staff is like a good marriage; you have some diversity, but your morals and values are similar.

At the top of the list of acceptable candidates should be someone who will do the right thing. This is probably an overused phrase, but that is our starting point. If your candidate requires a lot of rules around what "doing the right

The following essential qualities may indicate a new hire's potential to be a future leader. These traits follow the "servant-leader" model, the preferred route at Plante Moran. They are:

1. The ability to be trusted, to always have others' best interests in mind. People will then believe you will always do the right thing.
2. The ability to be receptive to others' points of view.
3. The desire to seek the truth and not settle for convenient answers.
4. The natural inclination to give credit away and to accept blame.
5. Keeping an eye on the world outside of your organization, to see where the world is really going and how your organization fits into that direction.
6. Optimism.
7. Humility—not taking yourself too seriously, not believing your own press clippings.
8. The constant focus on what's important—your clients—and helping staff to see that as well.

thing" means, you haven't got a good candidate. So we believe the No. 1 item for any potential recruit is integrity.

How do you recognize integrity? There are several ways. Asking situational and open-ended questions during interviews can combine with assessment testing to help determine a candidate's integrity level. But watching and listening may be one of your most effective tools. In an interview, an otherwise strong candidate might talk about skirting the edges of what's correct and acceptable. You'll want to know just how close to the line this candidate is willing to go without crossing it. Ask about challenging situations and how they handled them. Ask about their near misses and failures and steps they took to avoid failure.

Try to define other key qualities that are important to your particular business goals. In our firm, innovation and growth are important. How risk-tolerant or risk-averse the individual is may be an indicator of his or her ability to identify new opportunities or to process improvements.

It's important to define what kind of risk-taking you will accept in a candidate. One kind of risk-taking means taking a calculated risk, looking at new opportunities, and processing improvements that are predefined but don't gamble away what the business holds dear. In juxtaposition, there is risk-taking that's more extreme and asks the same integrity questions we just discussed: "Well, if we break the rules, nobody will care."

We want as much as we can get of the former risk-taking, not the latter. This is how new services, processes, or alliances are developed. We do not hire those willing to test the limits of ethics or laws.

Often, you just have to trust your gut and exercise judgment about where your candidates fall on the risk-taking spectrum. It's a mistake to think, "This is just an entry-level position," and overlook what your gut is warning you to consider.

These qualities build upon other must-have attributes: technical and professional competence, interpersonal skills, and the ability to collaborate and work on teams.

Nevertheless, all of the experience, instinct, and testing in the world won't guarantee you'll get perfect new hires, because that isn't realistic. Future leaders are created through formal training, life experience, maturity, and growth in a position. A person can have outstanding technical skills, but their life experiences help enrich their capabilities. One of the interesting facts about Plante

Moran leaders is that they were not hired necessarily for their leadership experience. They were identified early on as individuals who had potential, and that potential was nurtured and allowed to grow. Skills such as critical thinking and problem-solving will evolve with maturity and experiential learning, which we detail in Chapter Four.

Beyond these considerations, the performance management system we employ at Plante Moran identifies several personality traits that help evaluate staff members' potential:

1. **Enthusiasm and drive:** Approaches work passionately; has a strong desire to achieve success.
2. **Work ethic:** The willingness to work hard to achieve success.
3. **Initiative:** Searches for personal and professional challenges and takes ownership of one's own development.
4. **Judgment:** Uses non-verbal and verbal actions in evaluating situations; does not judge on external factors such as appearance, ethnic background, etc.
5. **Professionalism:** Strives to continually develop skills to exceed clients' service expectations.
6. **Reliability:** Meets deadlines; holds up his/her role as a member of a team.

When it comes to identifying potential leaders and successors, the growth cycle of your organization will determine which leadership skills are necessary. If you're in a startup phase, you will need potential leaders who are demanding, task-focused, more daring, risk-taking, and rah-rah. They need to be very clear or more direct in their approach.

As your organization matures, and you want to build upon the foundation in place, your growth may depend upon challenging existing patterns and practices and building new ones. In these cases, you need potential leaders who are more nimble and who can respond to growth and changing conditions very quickly.

Any parent who has more than one child knows how different their children can be. It's worth keeping this in mind when hiring. In his groundbreaking book, *The Triarchic Mind: A New Theory of Human Intelligence*, Oklahoma State University psychologist Robert J. Sternberg identifies three components of human intelligence, and how they act and interact for individual success. As one source sums it up: "The triarchic theory of intelligence is based on a broader definition of intelligence than is typically used. The ability to achieve success depends on the ability to capitalize on one's strengths and to correct or compensate for one's weaknesses. Success is attained through a balance of analytical, creative, and practical abilities."

Knowing that people have different mixtures of these qualities helps you figure out where they will function best in your organization. It's a matter of the right fit, and how the puzzle comes together for them.

Each kind of intelligence has its role, as well. Someone may be innately smart. That's good in many ways, but it may not be the best attribute, for example, if that person is responsible for developing others. Why? Because innate thinkers are often skip-thinkers. If a process takes 10 steps, they go from one, two, and then right to step 10. Staff trying to learn from them will be wondering, "What happened? I need to know what steps three through nine are."

Also crucial to the overall health and longevity of your organization is creating a talent pool that is deep enough to ensure a wide selection of possible leaders for succession. Be sure not to discount mergers or acquisitions because they often bring qualified, well-prepared leaders into organizations.

RECRUITING

Recruiting young people right out of college or technical schools requires different methods than finding experienced staff.

For the former, most firms recruit on college campuses, working closely with professors and the campus recruiting offices. Your company's website, Facebook page, and community involvement will all set the tone for information that is important to this group. You want a "look" on your website and in your materials that will appeal to them while staying consistent with your core brand. The campus recruiting offices will help you with the details, but understand that competition for the best students starts early, in freshman and sophomore years.

Once you have identified potential candidates through initial interviews, what happens next? One or more interviews with top leaders or departmental managers? Perhaps a generic test of some kind? That's not likely to guarantee consistently good results. Continuing the family analogy, if you consider job candidates to be potential members of your family, and thus people who must fit into your culture, a more thorough process is advised. Here are some suggestions:

Psychological assessment and testing.

Psychological testing and assessment may include an extensive interview with the firm's psychologist, or a contracted professional, followed by testing of the candidate's personality and cognitive abilities. The psychologist evaluates the test results and creates a report that presents the strengths of the candidate, areas of possible development, and whether or not the candidate should continue to be considered for employment.

Plante Moran uses assessment extensively when recruiting for all areas, other than campus recruiting. Technical testing can be used to evaluate a candidate's abilities in a number of areas, ranging from knowledge of basic or specialized software to their familiarity with job-specific tools and technology.

Interviews.

This all-inclusive term has many incarnations, but it is by far the primary tool to evaluate candidates. Every detail should be considered, including the composition of the interviewing team and how interviews will be conducted.

First, avoid the narrow, traditional course of having candidates interview with only management and senior management personnel. It's better and more effective when the interview team includes high-performing staff who will be the candidate's peers if they are hired. This also reinforces for current staff their value and contribution to the firm. A second round of interviews generally follows with more senior-level managers from areas involved with the position for which the candidate is being considered.

With young candidates, it's important to keep in mind they often do not have a comprehensive five-year plan, and when asked the traditional questions about their future, they might even say as much. This is normal, and should not automatically disqualify them. In fact, one current Plante Moran partner was hired even though he was extremely tentative about his future when he interviewed years ago.

"When I had my internship interview," he told us, "the partner asked me why I wanted to do this. I said, 'It's an experiment. I don't know what I want to do, but I need to find out what it's about and

Plante Moran's Challenge Event

For the past several years, Plante Moran has conducted a special recruiting event for college sophomores and juniors. Designed to expose talented young people to the field of public accounting, it also familiarizes them with the firm's culture. The weekend event, held at major hotel conference facilities, attracts students from many states. Part leadership program, part cultural experience, it also helps the firm identify talent earlier in the recruiting process.

Students participate in various activities, such as interacting with Plante Moran staff at all levels; participating in round-robin rotations on various subjects; and icebreaking activities, such as putting together bicycles in teams.

if it's something I want to do.' I didn't set out to become a partner when I walked in the door. I thought I'd be here two years, see how it goes and see if I liked it. After two years, I had made up my mind I wanted to move up to the next level of associate. When I did, I realized this would be my home for a long time."

A word about the younger generation of workers: Attracting and keeping this group—so-called "millennials"—requires some new techniques. Now at 70 million strong and 20 percent of the U.S. population, this group has been the subject of considerable study by business experts.

According to "Millennials in the Workplace: R U Ready?" published in Knowledge@W.P. Carey, millennials may require more coaching, for instance. "They're tech-savvy, nimble, enthusiastic, and achievement-oriented. Like all young people, they offer the corporate world enormous energy and talent. However, harnessing those positive attributes will take a patient, nurturing touch."

Consider the fact that studies indicate the top 20 percent of college graduates—that is, the very people you want to attract to your firm—won't work for companies that don't give them access to Facebook. That number will only increase.

Plante Moran recently was named by *Human Resources Executive* magazine as one of the 18 best companies for millennials to work for. When evaluating the things important to millennials, they cited:

- Management's actions match its words.
- Management shows appreciation for good work and extra effort.
- Management involves people in decisions that affect their jobs or work environment.
- Everyone has an opportunity to get special recognition.
- New staff is treated as a full staff member regardless of their position.
- Promotions go to those who best deserve them.
- People avoid politicking and backstabbing as ways to get things done.
- People look forward to coming to work.
- There is a "family" or "team" feeling.

The interviewing process can be grueling for candidates. Their ability to withstand the rigors and stay positive is yet another test of their suitability for professional careers.

BEHAVIORIAL-BASED INTERVIEWING

This style of interviewing is gaining popularity. It focuses not on what candidates have done in the past, but what they might do in the *future* based on what they have done in the past, either on the job or in other circumstances.

When hiring experienced staff, as opposed to campus hires, behavioral-based interviewing can be especially predictive of a candidate's skills, experience, and fit for a position within your organization.

Behavioral-based interviewing requires preparation. Certain competencies are identified for a particular position. Then, questions are developed to help determine if a candidate has displayed those competencies.

For example, to determine a candidate's problem-solving skills, Plante Moran might ask questions such as:

- Tell me about a time you were able to identify a problem and resolve it before it became a major issue.
- Tell me about a situation in which you were responsible for solving a problem that affected others in the organization. How did you involve them in solving this problem?
- Tell me about the last significant crisis situation you faced on your job. What did you do to get through this crisis?
- Walk me through a situation in which you had to solve a problem using multiple resources.

Using a Behavioral Based Interviewing Model, "Share." Developed by Novations Group Inc., here is a guide for developing questions for behavioral-based interviews:

S=Situation: What was the situation? Seek specifics such as names, dates, times, numbers, places.

H=Hindrance: What challenges or obstacles did you face in that situation?

A=Action: What actions did you specifically take to combat them?

R=Result: What was the end result/outcome?

E=Evaluation: What did you learn from the experience? What might you do differently next time?

HIRING EXPERIENCED PROFESSIONALS

You may find that your growing business has a need to hire people with experience versus staff right out of college. This may be the case if you are starting or expanding a service area.

All of the steps we talked about above still apply, but perhaps your greatest strength in getting the most capable individual is your personal and professional network. It is always helpful to invest time in meeting people well in advance of when you might work together. In the sales world, it's called "building a pipeline." We've never met a great sales manager who didn't have a list of two or three people they would hire today, if given the chance. These are people with whom they have met and whose work they have observed. They may even, in a casual way, have introduced them to a supervisor. The point is that the time to start looking for talent is way in advance of when you need it. We like to call initial talks with potential candidates "exploratory conversations." There is a clear understanding that there isn't a position open today, but you are just getting to know the candidate.

When you have openings for experienced candidates, your professional network may be the best resource. With today's technology, it never has been easier to put a post on LinkedIn or Facebook, or to send an e-mail asking for help filling an open position. We suggest you go to an outside recruiter only after these steps have been exhausted.

One other point to consider relates to references. In one of Jack Welch's books, he said that the hiring manager, not the Human Resources department, should always do the reference checks. This allows better insight into candidates and, potentially, better coaching decisions later on, if they are hired.

Finally, another practice to follow with experienced hires: We always try to meet the candidate we want to hire three times, preferably in three different settings, before we make an offer. This offers a better overall picture of the candidate. We can be more comfortable in investing time, training, and mentoring with such a candidate.

Recruiting for diversity is no longer an option if you want your business to thrive in the 21st century. Some data that underscores this reality: According to the U.S. Department of Commerce, minority-owned businesses in the U.S. grew by 35 percent between 1997 and 2002—a total of 4 million. Between 2002 and 2008, the estimated growth rate for majority women-owned firms was similar to majority men-owned firms (11 percent vs. 12 percent). Majority-owned, privately held, women-owned firms accounted for nearly 29 percent of all privately held firms in 2008, according to the National Women's Business Council.

In 2002, according to U.S. government sources, minorities owned 4.1 million companies that generated $694 billion in revenues and employed 4.8 million workers. Of minority-owned businesses: 39 percent are Hispanic-owned, 30 percent are Asian-owned, 27 percent are African American-owned, and 6.5 percent are Native American-owned.

Finally, diverse teams tend to outperform homogenous ones. Their wider range of creativity and ingenuity resulting from diverse backgrounds is increasingly valuable.

"There are a lot of different kinds of diversity. Clearly gender, race and ethnicity, and religion come to mind, but there is also diversity of thought, experience, and discipline. To me, when you're in a diverse environment, you're learning differently and producing a better result for your clients and staff. It's amazing how many times I've heard something at age 52 that I wondered, 'Where was I the first 52 years of my life because I haven't met this kind of person before?' I live in a neighborhood with many wonderful Middle Eastern families, and it's fun to sit down with friends I respect and compare different religious thoughts, different kinds of foods—just different ways of thinking and ways of looking at the world."

—Gordon Krater

One Plante Moran partner candidly described his feelings after going through the long application process a few years ago: "Getting in this firm might be harder than climbing Mt. Everest. You go through what feels like a hundred interviews, you get tested, you meet all these people. I remember being with the psychologist for three hours going over the test results, and thinking, 'All right. I like chocolate ice cream better than vanilla! What else do you want to know? I want to go home!' "

So there is a compelling business reason to attract the right staff and aim for diversity. If your organization isn't reflective of the business community, it will impact your ability to grow and expand.

We have encountered proof of this. A firm founded nearly 50 years ago by business people originally from Mexico was considering several firms, including Plante Moran, for professional services. This firm wanted to know how many minority-owned and female-owned businesses we already had as clients.

Because of our attention to diversity—which includes hiring diverse staff, the creation of a Diversity Council, and the use of tools such as the Diversity Continuum and Diversity Wheel—the answers to those questions came readily, and we won the client.

A more global example was Plante Moran's ability to win a client in China, when competing against several large competitors, including companies that also had deep roots in China. Our existing office in China and staff in the U.S. created a diverse account team to work on a proposal. Our China staff focused on language nuances, proposal translations and cultural traditions. All of this helped Plante Moran win the client.

Achieving diversity requires an organization to take several concrete steps:

• Define what you mean by "diversity," and write it down.

**Tips for managing
diverse talent:**

- Recognize differences in the way people work, think, learn, and deliver. Counsel staff to excel in their own way, not just the way you did.
- Provide mentoring.
- Emphasize communication and try to work through cultural barriers.
- Look for opportunities to be exposed to different cultures and learning styles.
- Avoid stereotypes, both positive and negative, and view staff members as individuals. Look for the individual's unique talents.
- Encourage diversity within work teams. This helps bring a different perspective to each situation.

"The work and messages our Diversity Council delivers are spot on. We recognize that we need to more closely mirror the society where we work. There are challenges to getting there. More than one firm is aggressively recruiting this field of candidates. I think we need to be appropriately aggressive without chasing after everyone just to make numbers. We follow our regular recruiting practices and try to recruit people we think are a good, long-term fit. Our diverse staff members seem to have developed informal networks within the firm and help to support each other. To me, this is a positive. It reflects the good job we have done asking our diverse staff to help us make Plante Moran a place they want to be. We cannot put ourselves in their shoes. In addition, we try to find ways to improve the chances of advancement through the team partner, buddy system, mentoring programs—again, just as we do with any staff."

—Beth Bialy

At Plante Moran, for instance, diversity includes not just gender, race or ethnicity, but also factors such as economic status, geographical location, marital status, religion, educational background, and more. Diversity of thought is important. To make sure you have diverse perspectives, we suggest identifying a few people in your firm who have a perspective different than yours, and who may even disagree with you, and ask these individuals for advice.

- Track your efforts toward diversity in recruiting.
- Consider appointing a committee to develop and monitor your company's diversity policies and progress.
- Consider involvement in community or academic institutions with activities focused on diversity.
- Identify and access various minority business or trade organizations.
- Report formally and informally about your firm's progress toward diversity.

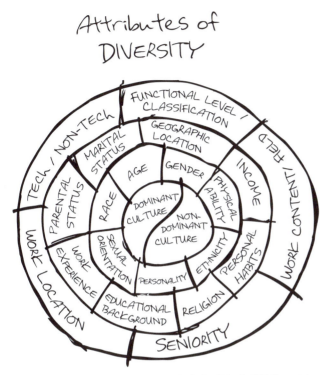

Attributes of Diversity

Implementing Diversity, Marilyn Loden, McGraw Hill Books, Burr Ridge, IL, 1996. By permission.

Attributes of Diversity: Plante Moran recognizes there are multiple attributes of diversity—including but not limited to age, gender, race, geography, marital status, and religion—that are so valuable to our firm and our clients. An inclusive mindset recognizes that diversity creates strong, creative businesses that attract the best and brightest talent and are better positioned to proactively address the changing work environment.

Diversity in leadership continues to be a challenge at some firms, and extra attention can make a difference. A diversity initiative helps develop people with diverse attributes for leadership positions in organizations and communities. You can't underestimate the importance of having diverse people in leadership positions. Without that, your so-called commitment to diversity is just lip service. You can have all the programs you want, but until you have some diversity in your leadership and partnership, there won't be enough people others can look to and think, "Yes, I can do that."

Onboarding New Staff

A first step in retaining new staff, and thus re-recruiting them, is an effective onboarding process. You want to make new staff feel at home as soon as possible and reaffirm their decision to join your company. According to the Aberdeen Group, 76 percent of firms now have a formal onboarding process as compared to just 40 percent in 2005. Firms that had strong onboarding programs had up to a 20 percent increase in retention and productivity. This

> **"Plante Moran is always re-recruiting talent.** When a great talent tells us they are thinking about a new opportunity outside the firm, we circle the wagons and have them talk to several partners and sometimes also management team members. We reinforce how much we love working with them and what a great performer they are. We are challenged to re-recruit on a regular basis, and growing our stars is a key performance measurement for partners."
>
> —Beth Bialy

research also shows that a majority of firms with successful on-boarding programs:

- Extend the onboarding programs to a new hire's first six months;
- Have managers responsible for the onboarding programs; and
- Incorporate socialization in the onboarding process.

Kelly Springer, a partner in the Grand Rapids, Michigan, office, remembers well why she stayed at Plante Moran after her internship in 1990. She saw that the culture that was marketed had proven to be "real" during that internship—and she was successfully recruited as staff. She found that people didn't just talk about caring, but really did care—about her, about clients, about their communities. It was more than a "sales pitch" to get her in the door.

Re-recruiting

What is there to retaining your staff beyond onboarding? Exactly what is "re-recruiting"? Star candidates and new hires require a lot of time, attention, and investment. Once they're on board, it's tempting to ease up some and take staff for granted. It's a temptation to avoid. Retaining staff is at times as big a challenge as attracting them.

Turnover costs a lot more than initial recruiting investments. Thus, "re-recruiting" is a valuable concept and practice. It involves developing and maintaining a close relationship with team members. It requires appropriately sized teams that allow supervisors to spend quality time with all team members. It requires they know the answers to basic questions, such as: Why do the team members work for your organization rather than another organization?

How do you judge the quality of these efforts in your organization? Your team leaders should have reasonable answers to the following questions—answers that would satisfy you if you were on their team:

- What are your staff members' top career concerns, and how are you working with them to address it?
- Do the team members believe they are fairly compensated?
- Do the team staff members' values align with your culture?
- Do the team members have enthusiasm and passion for the work they do?
- Can the team members achieve and maintain a balance between personal and professional responsibilities?
- Are the team members actively building their skills through learning and working on challenging projects?
- Have team members been asked what the organization can do to help them be more successful?
- Do the team members believe their manager and firm leadership care?

Another way to think about re-recruiting: Know what you might do if a valued staff member said he or she was leaving—and then do it now. Practices such as mentoring and career development are crucial to recruiting, and are detailed in our chapters on experiential learning and mentoring.

SUMMARY

1. Finding your future leaders begins with recruiting and hiring.
2. Look for those you think will fit into your culture.
3. At the top of the list of acceptable candidates should be someone who will always do the right thing.
4. Try to define other key qualities important to your particular business goals.
5. You may have to "trust your gut" and exercise judgment about your job candidates.
6. Don't expect the perfect new hire, because it's not realistic.
7. Personality traits useful to evaluate potential staff include:
   - Enthusiasm and drive.
   - A strong work ethic.
   - Initiative.
   - Judgment.
   - Professionalism.
   - Reliability.
8. When it comes to identifying potential leaders, the growth cycle of your organization will affect which leadership skills are necessary.
9. Knowing that people have different mixtures of qualities and kinds of intelligence helps you figure out where they will function best in your company.
10. Crucial to your organization's overall health and longevity is creating a talent pool that is deep enough to ensure a wide selection of possible leaders for succession.
11. Recruiting on college campuses requires working with professors and recruiting offices, as well as using social media.
12. Special recruiting events can enhance exposure of recruits to your company.
13. Once you have identified potential candidates, several steps should follow:
    - Psychological testing and assessment.
    - Technical testing.
    - Interviews. Avoid the narrow, traditional course of having candidates interview only with management. It's helpful to have staff with whom the candidate might be working interview them as well.

- Consider behavioral-based interviewing. This focuses not on what candidates have done in the past, but what they might do in the *future* based on what they have done in the past.

14. When hiring experienced professionals, the above steps still apply, but using personal and professional networks is effective as well. "Exploratory conversations" with potential candidates can clear the way for a future offer. LinkedIn and Facebook posts are another way to connect with experienced candidates.

15. Go to outside recruiters only after other steps have been exhausted.

16. The hiring manager, not Human Resources department, may do the reference checks.

17. Recruiting for diversity is no longer an option in the 21st century. There is also a compelling business reason. Surveys show diversity enhances creativity, ingenuity, and profits.

18. Achieving diversity requires concrete steps:
    - Define what you mean by "diversity," and write it down.
    - Diversity is multi-faceted and includes such factors as geographical location, religion, even "diversity of thought."
    - Track your efforts toward diversity in recruiting.
    - Consider setting up a diversity committee.
    - Consider involvement in community or academic institutions' activities on diversity.
    - Identify and access various minority business or trade organizations.

19. Onboarding programs are increasingly popular and are shown to increase retention and productivity.

20. Re-recruiting is key to retention of good staff. It involves developing and maintaining a close relationship with your team members. One way to think about this is to know what you might do if a valued staff member said he or she was leaving, and do it now.

"Often the reason a firm must merge with a larger firm is because they haven't developed the next generation of leaders. Good firms have developed the systems and processes to attract, retain, develop, and promote people. That's part of what keeps Plante Moran's culture together. Our first belief is to develop talent—because we attract great talent. We want to develop, retain, and promote them."

—Gordon Krater

"Three main areas of focus on staff are: Attract better talent. Retain it longer. Deploy it better."

—Bill Hermann

CHAPTER FOUR

Learning:
Formal, Informal, Experiential

Your success begins with your staff. But even the most talented staff needs the support of consistent, well-developed training—of all kinds.

Effective training requires a combination of formal and experiential learning. Coaching occurs in formal technical settings as well as through casual interactions. Suggestions and goals are discussed in formal career planning sessions and informally with mentors and others in leadership roles.

Training is offered to all and is intended to help everyone—whether or not they are destined to be top leaders—but it assumes that all staff may have leadership potential. In addition, good training programs and practices should relate and/or lead to business goals and tie directly to individuals' personal goals. Formal or technical training should be the base of increasingly sophisticated, integrated layers of learning, all building upon one another and culminating with a desired end: each staff member reaching his or her highest and best potential.

How do you institutionalize learning and help staff be all they can be? By developing formal, informal, and experiential opportunities and programs that begin early in staff members' careers and continue throughout their tenure. Mentoring, which underlies learning as much as culture underlies successful organizations, becomes more important as careers mature. It will be discussed in greater detail in Chapter Five.

Begin first with a staff development model—call it a roadmap to leadership, or a schematic for success. At Plante Moran, for instance, we have a tool called the "Pyramid of Progress." This foundational model is designed to help staff understand the process of developing their technical, relationship, and client-service skills. It identifies progressive steps that help guide staff to set the right goals. With each step, they build upon existing relationships and competencies while developing new ones.

The Pyramid helps staff measure their client service progress. It helps them know where they stand in their professional development, and what they need to do to improve. But the Pyramid can also apply to staff development. As a staff development model, the Pyramid identifies the competencies or building blocks that staff will develop in order to become high-performing client servers at the firm (those clients may be internal as well as external).

All of this sounds somewhat complicated at first. Your own developmental model should result from months or even years of work, reflection, and the input of many people and best practices. Perhaps most important, it also will reflect some common sense about how people in your organization learn and grow.

PYRAMID OF PROGRESS

The Pyramid of Progress is a foundational tool used to guide staff development, practice development, and client service. Bill Hermann helped identify the model, and he explains it, beginning at "Technical Skills."

"First, you need a foundation of technical knowledge. Our first responsibility to our clients is to be technically superior. As you evolve in your role and your technical capabilities grow, you earn the respect of clients and colleagues. This is where it all starts. If people don't respect your technical skills, they won't ever come to you with a question, and the rest is pointless. This is why we focus so heavily on technical training for new hires in their first three years.

"Once you have started to gain respect from your clients for your technical ability, they will start to come to you directly with a question, which leads to the staff person's need for good communication skills.

"So the client is seeing this combination: You're technically good, you communicate well, they've gotten to know you, and they have a sense of what you're about because you've communicated and developed a relationship. Now, the client has a problem that's off-point, but he still calls you because you've given such good advice. In answering, you then impart some insight.

"Insight then will put you in a position where the client will say, 'Whenever we talk, I get an insight and options for consideration, so I'm going to come to you more often when I've got a problem.' It doesn't matter what the problem is. And so you evolve into a problem solver.

"Problems can be solved with a product or service that you offer as a firm, or it can be introductions to other people outside of your firm. But the bottom line is the client comes to you. Once you provide solutions, then the client may ask your advice on a family problem or a community issue. You have become an advisor and, over time, a trusted advisor.

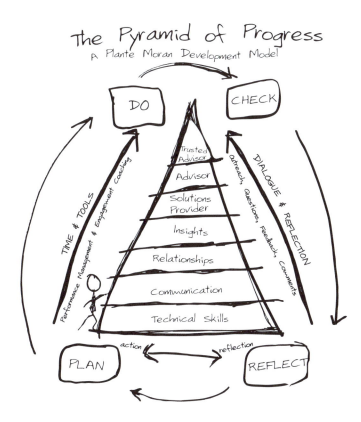

"As a trusted advisor, you'll be there no matter what the topic. That leads to practice development because these clients will talk to others about this great advisor they have, and say, 'Let me introduce you.' "

Some basic steps worth considering for your staff development model include:

Identify skills needed for all jobs, from entry-level to leadership. Plante Moran has identified a continuum based on the following skills. These skills are the foundation for career development and performance management. The firm also has defined behaviors that illustrate these skills for all staff members, regardless of their role in the firm.

Client/Relationship Management

- Developing effective client relationships and providing high-quality, professional service to our clients (internal and/or external) that results in a knowledge and understanding of client's needs and service that exceeds expectations.

Communication Skills

- Explains or conveys information to others through presentation, conversation, or written communication to gain support or causes others to take action; presents information to others in a pro-active or responsive manner and utilizes routine communication to build relationships.

Leadership/Management

- Leads/energizes others to pursue excellence and utilize their skills, while making significant contributions (on behalf of the client or firm); effectively utilizes and leverages skills, experience, and resources to manage tasks, projects, or practice.

Staff Development

- Builds and maintains positive relationships to achieve objectives; commits to develop and expand their abilities to improve performance and contributes to the development of others; practices the "Golden Rule" in all relationships.

Technical Skills

- Develops, understands, and applies specialized knowledge through experience, interaction with others, and formal training for the overall benefit of the firm; effectively utilizes appropriate technology to increase productivity and improve client service.

Network/Practice Development
- Contributes directly and indirectly to maintaining and growing the business.

Personal Qualities
- Enthusiasm and drive; hard-working; honest; initiative; good judgment; reliable; team-oriented and collaborative.

- Upholds firm philosophy and core values; acts as a role model and enhances firm culture and diversity initiatives daily; promotes a spirit that encourages diverse thought and creativity resulting in exceptional client service and staff development.

Provide necessary formal and ongoing learning opportunities.

Formal training can be provided in-house, by outside sources or institutions, or both. Universities and technical training programs offer formal training in leadership and other topics relevant to your firm's specialties.

Your own experts likely can provide training via webinars or online content. These can be shared with clients, if desired, which enhances your firm's profile as a leader.

Create an infrastructure that guides and supports each staff person.

Plante Moran calls this the Team Partner Structure and "Buddy Program." They anchor the entire acclimation and training process. It works like this:

- **Team Partner Structure.** New staff members are placed on a specific partner's team. That partner, along with other advisory team members, is responsible for creating the right professional growth and development opportunities for the new hire. The partner-to-staff ratio is purposefully kept low to ensure there is enough time to give the guidance the firm deems necessary for each staff person.

- **Buddy Program.** Each new staff member is assigned a "buddy" as well. The buddy usually has two to five years' experience with the firm and functions as a big brother or sister for the new staff. Buddies help new staff quickly acclimate and are available to answer questions that are crucial to interpret the culture and policies into everyday applications.

- **Apprenticeship Model/Focus and Choices.** Young staff members often don't know what precise direction or specialty to choose. They are exposed to a variety of experiences in different specialties or industries and, with help, they eventually learn where their strengths and interests lie. With guidance from their team partner and others on their advisory team, they can steer their careers toward the specialties that best suit their technical skills and interests.

Provide necessary on-the-job experiences.

Offer young staff chances to make brief presentations or to weigh in on certain decisions which may be outside of their normal role or level. Beyond the early career exposure experiences, staff continue to benefit by experiential learning as their careers develop.

For instance, Jim Proppe, Group Managing Partner and member of the firm's management team, told us about his early days working in the firm's Ann Arbor office. The Office Managing Partner at the time made sure to get Proppe some real experience.

"For a lot of assignments, he would just cart me around—that's really how I viewed it," Proppe said. "He'd take me to see a client with him, and I'd ask what he wanted me to do. He'd say, 'Nothing. Just be there.' I had been on the job maybe six months—I didn't know anything! And he knew that. But we'd go, and I'd sit there and watch, and listen and see how he handled the room.

"On the way back, we'd talk, and he'd say, 'OK, did you notice this, that? Did you see this, did you see that?' It was fantastic. I learned things like when to speak up, when to just listen, how to deal with controversy. I watched how he handled things, how he could be direct with clients when needed, or less so.

"After going with him on these client meetings on and off for about a year, he told me to lead the next client meeting. I told him I didn't know if I was ready. He said I'd do just fine. And I did. But if I messed up, I knew he had my back."

For managers offering these experiences, experiential learning and delegation are interchangeable; raising future leaders means letting go, bit by bit. But delegating comes with some risks. Giving a younger staff member a key role in a client presentation might result in a less than perfect, if not negative, presentation. Still, the senior staff is there to pick things up and move forward. In our experience, young staff members come through with flying colors at least 90 percent of the time. The preparation time might be out of sync for them at first. They may spend three days planning for a five minute presentation. That's OK. Now they have strength and confidence to know they can perform this particular task.

One Office Managing Partner believes that when developing staff, it's important to remember that they need time, attention, and care. She also cautions against "dumping" too much work on talented staff. The trick is to give them enough work to broaden their experience, but not so much that they'll burn out and become disenchanted with the entire profession.

Provide inside experience.

Potential leaders must be exposed to the inside issues that leaders encounter when running the firm or organization. This can include administrative assignments or opportunities to observe higher-level decision-making.

For instance, early in his career, one partner was put on a team to evaluate the firm's phone system, which was outdated, cumbersome, and didn't offer voicemail. A few senior managers had considered voicemail impersonal, and frankly had failed to understand as quickly as younger staff that it was the business tool of the future. The partner's team recommended using voicemail—at the risk of offending those senior managers. But his team was right, and the senior managers recognized that.

An example of observational learning: One senior manager had been with the firm only four or five years in the mid-1980s when he was allowed to sit in on a high-level meeting of partners who were discussing a potential, significant merger that would expand the firm's footprint in Michigan. He wasn't sure why he was even in the room, because the topic was very confidential.

"I was listening to them discuss the pros and cons and one of the partners said, 'I don't know that this is the right thing to do,'" this senior manager recalled. "And then he turned and looked at me and he said, 'What do you think?' That they asked for my opinion totally stunned me. I told them I thought it was exciting and would help us grow into a much larger firm. Another partner asked, 'Aren't you worried about our culture?' I answered something like, 'No, I think we can figure that out.' That was my view. I was going against what

Training Don't-Dos

It's important to remember some characteristics of poor training practices:

1. **One-dimensional learning.** Highly experienced staff, especially, need breadth, interpretation, and process introduced into their learning. Offer new experiences, thoughts, and knowledge in context and with broad perspective.

2. **20th century training.** Not all learning has to take place in conference rooms with presenters. Some training can be posted online or on webinars, so staff can access the information at different times via different electronic devices—and more than once if necessary.

3. **Boring speakers.** Training sessions can drag with speakers that are dry rather than dynamic.

4. **Long training periods without interactions or breaks.** Segments lasting longer than 20 to 30 minutes without breaks, dialogue or breakout sessions are ineffective. Attention spans expire quickly.

5. **Simple logistics gone awry.** Training rooms are too hot or too cold; there aren't enough breaks in day-long training programs; the food is bad; restrooms are too small or too far away.

6. **Out of date.** If it looks like it did in college, it probably isn't effective for adults who have developed preferences for their learning style and are now used to being more collaborative.

this partner had been saying. But I felt comfortable enough that what I said wouldn't be held against me."

It wasn't. That night, the partner who had doubted the benefit of the merger called this manager at home. He told him he was glad the manager had spoken up and that it had helped him change his mind. He encouraged him always to speak up. It was a great example of learning and encouragement.

In all phases of any learning programs, provide feedback as soon as possible.

"Dashboard time," or travel time from a client meeting, is a great time for feedback, as illustrated in the example given above. Such feedback often is cited by staff as especially helpful. Making a plan to drive together, even when it isn't the most direct route, will ensure that there are opportunities for these discussions to happen. Immediate feedback also is recognized as a best practice overall. Consider questions such as: How did the meeting go? What could we have done differently? What could you do differently next time?

Informal feedback discussions during lunch outings or even casual meetings at partners' homes are other opportunities for informal feedback and learning. This can involve not just middle level managers and partners, but top leadership.

Any feedback can backfire or fall flat if it is not reflective. Just bluntly correcting young staff isn't as effective as asking why they took a particular action. Try to determine what the process was. It may show they took certain steps out of order, which led them in the wrong direction. If they alter their process, they will alter the result. Also, when the leader asks for feedback from the staff first, it creates an environment of reciprocity.

Not everyone is destined for leadership—and that's OK.

Those who have one-dimensional skill sets are best focusing on delivering that service. Someone who is brilliant with clients might have poor management skills with fellow staff. Each young staff is on a journey of self-discovery that goes on for years. The right learning and experiences affect that journey.

The objective is for everyone to perform to their highest and best use. Once people are in that place, they will contribute the most, be recognized the most, and will be the happiest. At Plante Moran, we have some very talented people who have no management responsibilities; they are strictly client servers. And we celebrate that, because ultimately, that's what we're about—serving clients. We need to have an outward focus. So we've had some people who have been effective client servers, but for whatever reason, might not have been that good as managers. That's what creates an effective unit—people having to perform where they can be most effective and impactful. One senior level partner has helped mentor several Managing Partners but has not been considered for, or considered on his own, that role for himself. He is recognized as a model partner with enormous value to the firm. And he is the first to acknowledge he is in the perfect place for his skill set.

It's important to recognize that aspirations and skill sets don't always match up. The role a staff member wants to play in your firm may not be where he or she will best perform. Your organization needs to facilitate a win-win template for helping staff understand this basic tenet of professional development.

LEADERSHIP TRAINING AND EXPERIENCES

As more and more programs and experiential practices fall into place, a leadership program emerges. For instance, the Buddy Program benefits new hires—but it also requires fairly young staff themselves to train to be a buddy. Those who are a bit more senior train the buddies, and this progression goes on up the ladder. So learning in many forms benefits staff, clients and, ultimately, successful leadership transition because many staff will have had the benefit of multi-layered, integrated learning experiences.

For instance, those assuming their first in-charge roles learn such things as: How do you supervise? How do you train? How do you observe people? What should you be watching for? What have you learned about yourself? Are you a person that hovers over someone? Do you let the rope out so far that staff can fail? How do you get things at the right level?

This is what we refer to as "soft skill training." Once staff has foundational training, and as they move into more mature stages of development, they're prepared to become leaders. This layer of training is no longer technical, but more intuitive. It explores relationships, developing others, linking sound mentorship with client and practice success.

One-On-One Training Tips

1. Don't directly compare staff to their peers.

2. Be cognizant of the fact that everything you say, even off-the-cuff remarks, might be perceived as important to those you're training.

3. Avoid complaining about how busy you are. If you take a step back to count your blessings, it will put everything into perspective.

4. Don't assume everyone is at a point where they know that they want to be a partner. Thinking in terms of just getting someone to the next level will help them see the forest for the trees. Don't scare them off by wowing them with all the high-level partner stuff you are doing without letting them know how you learned to do it, who helped you, and how it was a progression.

Training for leadership is a never-ending subject of study in business. In an article entitled "Leadership Development: A New Business Imperative," Steven Gravenkemper outlined the case for developing leaders from within rather than hiring outsiders.

Main benefits were that future leaders thoroughly understand their firm's culture; potential leaders are more likely to stay with the firm if they see room for advancement. Gravenkemper advocated building a "leadership success template," wherein leadership skills, once identified, are linked to key business imperatives. Failure to do that risks development of skills that are either unrelated or in conflict with the firm's goals.

For individual learning and career action plans, Gravenkemper suggests four steps:

1. Be specific in targeting behaviors and action steps.
2. Be practical; apply new skills directly to work settings.
3. Offer direct feedback on newly practiced skills.
4. Follow up. It's critical to monitor progress, especially if direct supervisors are actively involved in such follow-up.

"Action learning" is an effective tool for developing future leaders. Typical steps of such programs include:

1. Senior executives create a cross-functional team of high-potential staff members.
2. Senior executives identify a current organizational challenge for the team.
3. The cross-functional team meets to receive its "action learning" assignment.
4. A facilitator introduces key principles of the assignment.
5. The team meets regularly and is given access to organizational resources needed to complete its assignment.
6. The action team presents its recommendations to the senior management team.

Gravenkemper conducted an additional survey of partners that helped identify exactly what helped them most as their careers progressed. Called the "Leadership Incubator Project," this initiative was aimed at understanding the key factors that contribute to developing firm leaders. The goal of the project was to identify

ON INCREMENTAL LEARNING

The "Pacer Theory" of learning goes like this: A beginner is better off taking smaller steps, or learning a bit at a time. The idea is to move at a pace within your comfort zone, but also be stretched enough that you learn, get comfortable, and get ready to learn some more.

Originally, the Pacer Theory referred to research on animal behavior. A pacer is a stimulus whose complexity is slightly higher than the animal's complexity level. When an animal interacts with a pacer, the preferred complexity level of the animal moves toward that of the pacer. Thus the animal's complexity level keeps rising as its experience with pacers increases.

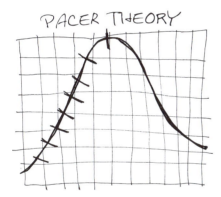

Applied to humans, this theory reinforces the idea that skills are built most effectively in incremental steps represented on the illustration above. Using the normal distribution curve, you would place, say, a beginning tennis player on the left side of the curve. In order to get better, it's far more effective for that player to compete against someone who is just ahead of them on the left side of the curve, rather than a professional, way over the right of the curve. If the beginner plays the professional, there is too much risk that he will give up and get discouraged because the difference between him and the professional is just too large.

So gradually over time, you improve your skills. Important in this process is a mentor or teacher, showing the way.

common best practices that might be helpful in developing future leaders. Findings also would be helpful to partners as they engage in staff development activities. The survey involved interviews with successful partners who identified these top factors as those most helpful to them in career advancement:

- Future partners were pushed outside their comfort zones with "stretch assignments."
- Future partners were exposed early on to partner mentors who became both coaches and sponsors for these individuals.
- Partner mentors spent a great deal of quality time with future partners.
- Practice development activities and skill-building were emphasized early in careers.
- "Real time" feedback was provided on a consistent basis.
- Future partners were open to receiving feedback and then acting upon it.
- Partner mentors generated a sense of excitement by effectively communicating a shared office or industry vision.
- Future partners worked closely with multiple partners on a variety of projects.

Leaders Shaping Leaders

"Bill Hermann was very intentional about identifying people and getting them the proper experience so that when the time came for his replacement, there was a pool of people who had had enough of the right kinds of experiences and mentoring to replace him. Today, as Managing Partner, I'm following Bill's model. I've been very intentional about getting different and diverse people different kinds of experiences so when the time comes for me to step aside, we'll have many candidates to choose from to replace me—and to carry on the Plante Moran tradition of succession."

—Gordon Krater

The overarching theme is that team partners make other team partners. It can be compared to an apprenticeship model in which the master craftsman and the apprentice work side-by-side. The master guides the apprentice in his or her learning, offers critiques and mentorship, and guides their learning by working "elbow-to-elbow." The next chapter explores in more detail the dynamic, often pivotal impact of mentorship.

SUMMARY

1. Even the most talented staff needs training of all kinds, both informal and formal.
2. Good training programs and practices should relate and/or lead to business goals and tie directly to an individual's personal goals.
3. You should create a staff development model to guide your training programs. It should be a foundational model designed to help staff understand the process of developing their technical, relationship, and client service skills.
4. Some basic steps for such a model include:
   - Identifying skills needed for all jobs, entry-level to leadership.
   - Providing necessary formal and ongoing training.
   - Designating a person for each new hire that can answer questions, and just be there. This can be called a Buddy Program, and evolves into an apprenticeship model.
   - Provide necessary on-the-job experiences.
   - Provide "inside" experience, allowing staff to see the workings of higher level staff.
   - In all phases of training, provide feedback as soon as possible.
   - Not everyone is destined for leadership. This does not mean they cannot find their perfect place in your organization and be appreciated for it.
   - "Soft skill training" places staff in positions where they must make more complicated decisions about people.
   - Individual career plans should target specific behaviors and action steps; be practical and apply new skills directly to work settings; offer direct feedback on newly practiced skills; and allow for follow-up.
   - "Action learning" is an effective tool for developing future leaders. Staff are given challenging projects and supported through the process of accomplishing them.

"Part of mentoring is painting visions for young staff. If you take a look at the development continuum of our leaders, there always was somebody painting a picture and showing us how to use our skills to be successful."

—Bill Hermann

"Our job is to develop staff so they can be successful here and in the community."

—Gordon Krater

"Mentoring is helping good leaders become great leaders."

—Tom Doescher

CHAPTER FIVE

Mentoring, Goal-Setting, and Measuring

Anyone who has had a great mentor knows it's almost impossible to quantify the value of such a relationship. In his book, *Coaching and Mentoring*, author Richard Luecke describes mentoring as "a means of developing human resources. Mentoring is about guiding others in their personal quests for growth through learning."

More informal and relationship-oriented, mentoring, Luecke continues, is a crucial component of staff development, the "day-to-day, manager-employee (and executive-manager) interactions that fortify skills, expand knowledge, and inculcate desirable workplace values."

Suffice it to say mentoring is an imperative business tool. Myriad surveys prove the benefits of both formal and informal mentoring programs. In 2005, Marilynne Miles Gray, of Mentoring Solutions Inc., completed a comprehensive study on mentor programs, and one of her findings showed that half of 378 U.S. companies surveyed either had formal mentoring programs or planned to establish them within a year.

One staff member of a firm
was bright and had one of the
highest grades in the state
on his technical certification
exams. He had great energy and
talent—but he also had poor
verbal grammar. He used about
a dozen words incorrectly, and
it was noticeable. Rather than
disqualify him immediately from
advancing, his mentor could
clearly see his potential, so the
two developed a plan. At first,
the mentee was sent to a formal
speaking class, but it had little
effect. So the mentor, with the
mentee's willing acceptance,
set up "nagging rights" for the
mentor. As soon as the mentor
heard his mentee misspeak in
any conversation, he corrected
it—immediately. The mentee
agreed he would always accept
the correction, and they would
move on. The corrections never
took place in front of clients.

Receiving immediate
feedback like that helped, the
mentor reported. The mentee
was mature enough to accept
the help, and his mentors were
open enough to offer help that
was quick, immediate, and raw.

It was also effective. The
mentee is now in senior
management, and rarely makes
a grammatical mistake.

The most important reasons for offering these mentoring programs were to:

- Enhance career development.
- Improve leadership/managerial skills.
- Develop new leaders.
- Put high-potential individuals in the fast career track.
- Promote diversity.
- Improve technical knowledge.

Other surveys and articles, Gray reported, listed other reasons mentoring is a must:

- Most companies report mentoring increases retention.
- Staff who had mentors report greater job satisfaction.
- Professionals who have had mentors earn more than those who did not.
- Many CEOs report that formal mentoring programs help women advance.
- Staff learn the ropes and unwritten rules more quickly.

Finally, one survey Gray cited showed that protégés—or mentees—said mentoring helped them feel valuable to their firms; tested their leadership and management skills; made them more objective and more promotable; and helped them decide to stay with their organizations longer.

The message could not be clearer: If your firm does not have some type of mentoring program, consider establishing one. Our mentoring programs at Plante Moran are long-established and were specifically highlighted in Maureen Broderick's 2010 book, *The Art of Managing Professional Services*. These programs begin with the more structured approaches, such as the Buddy Program, and evolve into leadership training exercises, where mentees and mentors learn more about themselves and their potential as they ask for help and, in turn, provide it to others.

Creativity, individuality, and imagination often play a part in the relationship between mentor and mentee. Here are some examples gathered from professional service firms:

- One mentor observed that his mentee was extremely critical and focused on what was wrong more often than what was right. The mentee was given the task to find people doing something right twice a week—and to tell them so. He had to report back to his mentor once a month on his progress.

- A mentee who consistently undersold his own contributions to his company was assigned to keep a written list of the good things he did on a monthly basis. He complained about how hard it was—at first. By the end of the year, he had a list of 75 items—and much better self-worth.
- One woman, now a successful partner in her firm and who leads important committees, was extremely shy early in her career. She could not even make eye contact with colleagues. Her mentor and others at her firm gave her consistent, candid, and timely feedback, and placed her in sink-or-swim situations. Today, no one would recognize the shy person she was before. Said her mentor: "She deserves all the credit; we just enabled her. She made all the changes."

The primary benefit mentoring offers is the attribute most needed: life experience. The experience that you get just by dealing with life absolutely plays a role in how you develop as a leader. You won't develop effective leadership skills until you've had a few hard knocks, faced problems, failed or taken chances. There are always people on your staff who are intellectually, technically, and interpersonally ready to become partners. But they may not have life and interpersonal experiences to round out their abilities. Higher-level leaders are expected to be able to respond in certain situations. If they've never seen these situations before, they won't have the empathy, or the confidence, required. You might freeze, panic, or just do the wrong thing.

Mentoring can be formal—when a mentor is assigned to a staff member—or it can be informal, where a staff member asks a senior manager to enter into a mentoring relationship. It's important to make appropriate choices in this relationship. As mentors begin their work, they should keep three goals in mind. These are to be:

- Innovative in thought.
- Principled in intent.
- Intentional in actions.

Mentors have a responsibility to deliver the best "just-in-time" advice and direction to their mentees, depending on the skills they

> **"One assignment I worked on with one of my mentors related to a city that had won a lawsuit appeal reimbursement for $1.7 million.** Since they had originally paid for the suit with a special tax levy, they now had to repay the taxpayers, several years later. It was very complicated; properties had changed hands, thousands of checks had to be calculated, processed, and mailed, and a dispute process needed to be established. I clearly remember sitting in the clients' offices and my mentor telling me to work through it and do whatever I thought would be appropriate. The fact that he had the confidence that I would get it right really motivated me to step up."
>
> —Beth Bialy

need to nurture at a given time. They also will need to bring discipline and dedication to their role. That means following up with the mentee and holding them accountable to the development paths that he or she will follow.

Mentoring, of course, is a two-way street. The best mentees need only have a few qualities: the ability to ask for, and to receive, honest feedback; to articulate what they would like to learn; to listen; and to apply what they're learning to their career development.

At Plante Moran, we identify mentees in various ways. All exhibit the ability for advancement and have a certain level of maturity. They may also benefit from a different point of view. In some cases, staff show so much potential early on, it's important to get them immediate input so they'll have a better chance to gain the skills needed for top-level leadership.

Mentoring relationships also result when someone seeks higher level managers as mentors. The key is to avoid looking like you're too busy to be approached. Also, it's important to make sure not to accept a mentee when you know another manager is perhaps better attuned to their area of expertise.

Plante Moran managers with substantial mentoring experience have identified the following qualities of a good mentor:

1. Good mentors set high standards.

2. Good mentors are transparent. They explain what they are doing and clearly discuss why they make certain observations about mentees or give certain assignments. One long-time partner was a mentor to many at Plante Moran over the years, including a current unit leader. This partner has long-since re-tired, but the unit manager still recalls the impact the mentor had on him—and why. "He was very open, very transparent. He talked about his personal life, both good and bad. He taught me that one way to get people to know and trust you is to share some of your screw-ups and travails in life." This mentor even conducted an informal career planning session at his home, by the pool, as the two ate lunch and relaxed. His young mentee couldn't believe it.

3. Effective mentors recognize the right time to offer key advice. We're all good at identifying what's wrong. We're not always good at helping fix it. So the best people-developers are good at helping people fix things. Human nature often leads people to think things will take care of themselves over time. Yet some never do.

One partner with nearly 40 years at Plante Moran worked with a new staff member who was talented but extremely competitive. This new staff member's family experience had programmed him to be this way. The mentoring partner recognized this, but he knew he had certain things he needed to tell this young staff mem-ber—and he knew he had to do so in the right way. If the mentee sensed he wouldn't make partner, he would leave, and the mentor didn't want to trigger that. So he waited and waited—until he saw just the right moment to raise the issue. The young staff member benefited from this feedback, and eventually made partner.

4. Effective mentors recognize and articulate gaps in a mentee's experience or knowledge, and suggest the right experiences to fill those gaps. One of our up-and-coming managers filled a gap in his experience when he was given the assignment to oversee a merger—from start to finish.

Another senior partner thought some of the younger lead-ers in the firm might benefit from sitting in on senior managers' monthly phone conferences. The senior managers covered some very sensitive, often strategic issues in these conversations. The senior partner wanted younger staff to see and hear how issues were tackled and decisions were made. But the senior manager also wanted feedback from his young group. He asked them for their thoughts, points of view—fresh ideas, without fear of reprisal. "Don't let us brainwash you," is how he put it.

When one of these young partners said very little in two meetings, the senior partner told him he didn't believe he didn't have some opinions. He instructed the younger staff member that if he didn't speak up in the next meeting, he would be thrown off his particular leadership team. Since then, the young staff member has been a great contributor.

5. Good mentors love to help, and step in when necessary. Giving mentees opportunities to try new things and to stretch themselves is important, but mentors need to be ready to intervene in case things go a bit sour. A big part of experiential learning is that if something goes wrong, the mentor can step in, take responsibility, and be a safety net to prevent the mentee from being destroyed by a mistake. One experienced mentor calls himself a "compulsive helper." He loves to help mentees succeed, and enjoys seeing these mentees become mentors themselves. That is what usually happens in a good mentor-mentee relationship. Helping becomes contagious.

6. Good mentors are good judges of their mentees' potential. Understanding what a mentee is capable of doing is crucial to that mentee's success. That helps the mentor guide the mentee on the right path, and away from unrealistic expectations or from positions that might make the mentee miserable.

7. Effective mentors are not overly nurturing or overly harsh. Mentors who are extremely competent may inadvertently be too hard on mentees who are slower to progress and to understand steps along the way. To such mentors, it's: "Just do it." Other mentors might be the opposite—too nurturing and coddling, so the mentee never moves along in his or her career path.

8. Effective mentors are honest and candid. As we said in an earlier chapter, one of our favorite sayings is "candor is kindness." An example here: One mentee had awkward, sloppy eating habits. At lunches with his mentor and colleagues, it was impossible to ignore. His mentor confided to a colleague he was going to bring this up with his mentee. The colleague was skeptical because it was so personal and sensitive. Yet, the mentor also knew that it was the kind of detail that could derail the mentee's career. So he mentioned it, and got a surprising answer. The mentee told him his father had advised him to eat with his left hand so he could take notes with his right. The mentee was right-handed but had followed his father's advice. He thanked his mentor for mentioning it and changed his eating habits.

> **"My first mentor believed in giving you stretch assignments.**
> And the best mentoring experiences were when my mentor allowed me as early as possible to experience things that were outside of my comfort zones, which pushed me to display more leadership. He always challenged me to work at a higher level, analyze situations carefully, and focus constant attention on clients. He gave me increasing responsibility for firm-related assignments with which he needed assistance. These projects really taught me about how the firm worked from the inside, and this early exposure I think piqued my interest in becoming an Office Managing Partner."
>
> —Kathy Downey

9. Good mentors let mentees know that they aren't expected to know everything. We try to emphasize that no one is expected to know everything and that learning and improving are lifelong processes. We tell new partners that the worst mistake they can make is telling themselves that they should know everything. There's no shame in asking for help to improve an area of weakness. Learning and improving is a lifelong experience, and even senior leaders ask for and receive help all the time.

Mentoring in Difficult Situations

Despite everyone's best efforts, sometimes it becomes obvious that a staff member or partner would be better somewhere else. This doesn't mean either party has failed; it just means a particular staff member would probably be happier somewhere else—and must be told this fact. How you handle such potentially delicate situations is as important as any other, and you go right back to your core values.

One now-senior partner was asked by his mentor to witness the process of separation when he was a fairly new partner. His mentor told him he was inviting him to do this because he knew the new partner would one day have to face this scenario.

The senior partner reviewed with his mentee his list of thoughts he had drawn up about why the partner would be happier in another firm. During the meeting, the partner who was struggling to fit in was invited to discuss all of the aspects of his situation, and agreed in writing with the terms of his separation from the firm.

Even this scenario, though, had come after a long period of preparation. It's the exception rather than the rule that anyone is let go and leaves in one or two days.

> **"When you look at where people should be in management, it varies according to their personality, disposition, skills, and a host of other personal factors.** Some folks excel in clearly defined situations while others prosper when the circumstances are vague and they have to figure things out. Some people thrive when their innovative skills are tapped. You just take a look at the spectrum of people and skills, find the highest and best use, put those people in those spots, and let them go."
>
> —Bill Hermann

In most cases, when a staff member may not seem fit for public accounting, it's more a matter of, "We have to part ways. How can we help you?" A staff member still has great accounting skills and could be effective with other companies. Plante Moran in some cases even offers assistance, sending out "feelers" to other firms for possible openings for the departing staff member.

GOAL-SETTING AND CAREER PLANNING

As informal as a mentoring relationship can be, it has a mission: to advance the mentee's skills and career development as far as possible. Effective mentors recognize there is no such thing as one-size-fits-all when it comes to helping mentees set goals and grow. Setting and measuring goals is therefore at the heart of the mentor-mentee relationship.

In *Alice In Wonderland*, Alice asks the Cheshire Cat, "What road do I take?" The Cat replies, "Where do you want to go?" Alice says, "I don't much care where." So the Cat tells her, "Then it doesn't matter which way you go."

In order to set career goals, it does matter. You need to know where you want to go. In general, the process is fairly straightforward:

- Set specific goals. Make sure they are realistic. If a mentee's own goal or vision is unrealistic, show them the skills and steps they'll have to take well before they can reach their vision.
- Communicate these goals. A mentor and mentee need to be very clear about goals. They should be in writing, but also discussed. The mentee should be able to repeat accurately back to the mentor exactly what the agreed-upon goals and expectations are. At the end of his career planning sessions, one partner repeats what he thought he heard, just to be sure he heard correctly and understood what he needs to work on.
- Set concrete steps to reach these goals. Often the mentee's vision of where they want to be is many levels beyond his or her current skill set. The mentor's job is to design a way to help the mentee reach that vision step-by-step, success-by-success. Without such steps, the gap between where the mentee is and wants to be may be so large, the mentee will give up for fear of failure. Help identify for a mentee where they might be in five years, and then what they can do each year to attain that destination. Recognizing that it's a three-year or five-year journey means they won't feel overwhelmed and doubt their ability to achieve that ultimate vision.
- Pay it forward. In review sessions with mentees, focusing on next year's goals along with reviewing last year's performance is more productive and inspirational to mentees than just measuring accomplishments, or the lack thereof, of the past year.

Bill Hermann's Definition of Accountability

"Accountability to a plan doesn't make us less professional, less caring, or less flexible. It defines success, calibrates results (versus measuring effort), creates opportunities to celebrate, stimulates teamwork, creates focus, and allows us to optimize our efforts. All delivered in moderation."

- Hold mentees accountable. Mentors only guide mentees. The mentee is responsible for his or her own development and advancement. If mentees don't report back, they must be approached and asked about their progress.

With a strong mentoring program in place, your firm has taken a significant step toward ensuring there is a qualified, prepared group of potential candidates who can assume top leadership roles. These candidates will have confidence in their abilities and in your firm's continuing, strong network of support.

SUMMARY

1. Mentoring is an imperative business tool. Surveys show more and more companies employ mentoring programs to enhance career development, improve leadership and managerial skills, develop new leaders, and put high-potential staff on a fast track.

2. Mentoring programs promote diversity, improve technical knowledge, and increase retention.

3. Those who received mentoring report that it helps them feel valuable to their firms, it tests their leadership and management skills, and makes them more promotable.

4. The primary benefit of mentoring is giving staff much-needed life experience.

5. Mentoring can be formal—when a mentor is assigned to a staff member—or informal, when a staff member requests such a relationship with a senior staff.

6. Mentors should be innovative in thought, principled in intent, and intentional in actions.

7. Steps to good mentoring include:
- Offer a reaching vision for a mentee's future career. Don't advocate an unrealistic career goal, too broad of a goal, or allow a mentee to set such goals.
- Create concrete steps to that vision.
- Get buy-in from the mentee. Successful mentorship programs are driven by the mentee's desire, not the mentor's.
- Don't be afraid to stretch mentees.
- Offer feedback on what someone is doing well, as well as what they need to improve.
- Offer encouragement.
- Conduct mentoring sessions informally and/or in locations that are more relaxing than the office conference room.

8. Mentors help staff set career goals. In these sessions, they should:
- Set specific goals.
- Communicate these goals.
- Set concrete steps to reach these goals.
- Focus on goals for the year ahead in review sessions as well as past performance.
- Hold mentees accountable.

"I had been with the firm about a year when co-founder Frank Moran stepped down as Managing Partner. Everyone was taken by surprise. One of my mentors said, 'This is going to be one of the best things to happen to Plante Moran.' I responded, 'How can you say that?' He said, 'A lot of firms our size in Michigan will disappear because the founder won't turn over the reins at an early enough age.' He was right—and it was Frank who set that template, turned it over, and allowed others to succeed him. The firm has survived and thrived ever since."

—Gordon Krater

"A lot of people have been leading their firms for a long time. I intentionally stepped down as Managing Partner when I did because I thought it put us in a better succession position. I'd have loved to have stayed on for another couple of years, but I thought it was better for the firm to have a change, and to focus on getting things ready for the next 20 years."

—Bill Hermann

"Best-in-class organizations emphasize succession planning as an ongoing process, not a one-time event. Leadership development becomes an ongoing dialogue. Such processes create a talent pipeline that produces leaders as needed. Event-driven succession plans often result in a reactionary or crisis-management approach."

—Steve Gravenkemper

CHAPTER SIX

Transition

So, your firm's culture is set. Potential leaders have been identified and given experiences that prepare them for top leadership. The process has been inclusive and transparent, and there is a cadre of candidates ready and able to assume command. It's time for transition, right?

Not entirely. One misstep in the final stage can derail the entire process: how and when the current leader decides to step down. As simple as it sounds, it is not. And many firms have run into problems at this critical stage of the succession process.

Consider the following less-than-desirable succession scenarios:

One rocky transition began with a father who had built up a company. He was entrepreneurial in nature, and was handing down the business to his son. His son's focus was building the organization—a skill the company needed at the time.

Unfortunately, entrepreneurs often have trouble letting go. The father did indeed hand down his business to his son and, on paper at least, "walked away."

But every time his son made a major decision or delegated significant work to others, his father made his objections known to all. This cast doubt on his son's authority.

This continued for more than a year, and the business drifted. The son finally told his father to keep his advice to himself. It was hard, but the end result was that the business began growing again and ushered in a new era.

In the case of one major firm with a global presence, a very strong leader had been responsible for the company's explosive growth. When the leader stepped down, there was confusion because this leader had been dominant for so long. In a 2009 *Forbes* magazine article, "Succession Planning: How Everyone Does It Wrong," Stephen A. Miles wrote: "When the departing chief executive officer has had a strong run, there is worry about his successor's ability to maintain the momentum." Conversely, Miles added, when a CEO has "performed poorly, there's anxiety about whether and how fast his successor will be able to correct course."

In another case, one leader planned to announce his departure two years in advance of the actual event. That left the organization with a lame duck leader and a new leader serving simultaneously. People did not know who to consult or who really was in charge.

The beginning of successful succession starts with the leader, assuming there is no crisis, such as when a CEO or Managing Partner is removed by the board of directors or designated committee. Here are some considerations for the process of transition:

Know when it's time for a change in leadership.

Being a good leader means knowing when to get in, and when to get out. And the commitment to getting out is hard. You have to recognize that change is good. So the decision to give up leadership is as difficult as deciding who should take over leadership. It's a big part of the transition issue—and may be the most difficult of decisions.

Again, there must be a realization that the change is right for the organization. If a leader does not truly believe this, he or she may stall the change and then abruptly step out and leave a gap. The current leader must be willing to move out of the role as the new leader takes over, much like the hand-off of the baton in a relay race. Coordinated overlap is healthy. The goal is to be ready and committed to what you're doing. Then, if you're the outgoing leader, you get out of the way or, if you're the new leader, you dive in full speed.

Knowing it's time to step down varies with the individual, but the decision may also depend on where your organization is in its life cycle. At Plante Moran, we have seen previous Managing Partners switch focus to concentrate on what needs attention at the time they assumed leadership. One Managing Partner was focused externally on business growth; his successor invested more time with internal processes. If you are the current leader, you may recognize that the next era for your business requires skills that aren't necessarily your strengths, and stepping aside makes sense because it's the right time. Leaders themselves may also come to the realization they need new stimuli, a new focus, and find a different role within their own organizations.

Finally, if you have a strong culture and leadership process, you can be confident that a good field of candidates is ready to step into the leadership role.

Stepping aside at appropriate intervals makes room for others to advance through your corporate structure.

How long should a leader remain in charge? We suggest about eight to 10 years, because that is not quite a generation, and it allows enough time to develop the next generation. At the same time it demonstrates to the next generation that there is ample time for them to move and grow in the organization. Other organizations may recommend 20- or 25-year increments. In our opinion that's too long for most firms, especially with the ever-changing technical and technological aspects of business today. It stymies the development of future leaders because they may be locked out of advancement. They may even look elsewhere for their next opportunity if there is no prospect for movement.

It really boils down to what's best for the organization. You may love being the CEO, president, or Managing Partner. You may know you would be re-elected or accepted for another term or several more years. Instead of considering this, think of the future of your firm and recognize that it may be time for someone else to lead. If this is the case, you should encourage a graceful transition.

Myriad other problems can result when a leader refuses to make room for a successor. One leader hung around so long, his firm's board of directors decided it was time for him to look for a successor. He hand-picked his successor, but the board members selected someone else. As the succession took place, the outgoing leader called the incoming leader into his office. The new leader assumed it was to wish him good luck and perhaps to offer some good advice.

On Visibility

"We ended up having 13 partners assume new leadership roles when I stepped aside as Managing Partner.
That gave 13 people new areas for growth. They were excited, they were energized, and since then they have been the catalyst for significant change. I think other partners and staff are looking and saying, 'Hey, that means I can make a change if I get to that role,' and they start thinking, creating. It's great for your firm's long-term future development."

— Bill Hermann

Instead, the outgoing leader admonished him and lamented the rejection of his hand-picked successor. The entire scenario cast a bitter end for one leader and a bitter beginning for his successor.

Outgoing leaders can pave the way for their successors by getting difficult challenges and battles out of the way.

In 1999, Plante Moran launched the most exhaustive strategic planning exercise in its history. It was a time of harder-than-normal transition. The planning addressed the firm's governance structure and the way decisions were made. Creating a proposed structure and effectively communicating its benefits to the partnership was an extensive undertaking. The outgoing Managing Partner's decision to finish this process before he left helped his successor avoid beginning his new role facing divisive decisions or controversy.

Establish a democratic process for picking successors.

Because of their ownership structure, most professional service firms have unique governance characteristics to consider when selecting new firm leaders. It's important to have a process that includes the partners in the selection so that the decision reflects their interests. Appointing a hand-picked successor should be avoided; it doesn't allow for input from the partners. The process should be as inclusive as possible.

In her book, *The Art of Managing Professional Services*, Maureen Broderick reported that in her survey of professional services firms, a surprising number—46 percent—still had no established succession plans or processes. Those that did have some kind of plan employed mechanisms such as leadership development groups, management committees, and the like.

We've developed the following suggested steps for establishing a succession planning process:

- Develop criteria for filling key positions.
- Assess individual candidates against these criteria.
- Create individualized leadership development plans for internal candidates.
- Identify gaps that may need to be filled by external hires.
- Conduct ongoing reviews of the timing of anticipated key position openings.
- Develop metrics, such as retention of top talent and percentage of positions filled internally versus externally.
- Facilitate an annual talent management review process.

Plante Moran's structure for succession reflects the firm's inclusive culture, which helps partners feel they have input and influence over the final selection. Their involvement also tends to surface new and creative ideas and identification of new areas that need growth or attention.

There are various ways to approach leadership selection, but whatever process is used, it should be as democratic and inclusive as

> **"The nominating committee process takes the pressure off of possible successors.** This is not a political process, where you run for this office. I may want to do the job, but that's not my choice, it's the nominating committee's choice. So I didn't have to do any coalition-building or lobbying. As a matter of fact, I was just silent. When people asked me about it, I said, 'If that's what the firm decides, I'd love to do it.' That was the extent of the conversation I had."
>
> —Gordon Krater

**BEST PRACTICES IN
SUCCESSION PLANNING**
- Start early.
- Solicit input from key stake-holders.
- Create a leadership success profile.
- Identify criteria for filling key positions.
- Assess internal and external candidates on these criteria.
- Develop a transition plan for new leaders.
- Conduct an annual review of top talent.

possible. Ideally, there should be several choices for the next leader and, if possible, no surprises.

Plante Moran employs a nominating committee made up of members elected by the partners. When the current Managing Partner signals he or she will not be running for another term, the committee surveys partners, well ahead of time, about the kind of attributes they think a new leader should possess.

Responses are accumulated, and partners are asked to suggest candidates for consideration. In the last leadership transition, there were many names, but three or four were multiple vote receivers. Next came a series of interviews. The nominating committee narrowed the list, recommended candidates for the vote, and the vote was taken.

The current Managing Partner or leader should be careful not to influence or compromise the process. His or her primary role is to make sure there are enough people who are ready to assume top leadership and allow the process to do the rest.

And so the process went forward again at Plante Moran—with minimal disruption of the firm's priorities and business operations. The smooth transition in and of itself is noteworthy. However, the process that precedes it has a positive effect on all who observe it.

Says Jim Proppe, Plante Moran's Group Managing Partner: "As I look back and reflect on each of the Managing Partners and their management teams, I think they did a phenomenal job setting up the next group. We know of other firms where they've had absolute knock-down, drag-out battles. Somebody emerges from that, bloodied, as the next Managing Partner. And then the direction of the firm changes significantly. The fact that we have avoided those situations has led to successful transitions and a great job of preparing the firm for the next generation of leaders."

SUMMARY

1. Successful succession begins with a current leader's decision to step down. This is not easy to do. Leaders need to recognize when it's time for a change in leadership, and that change is right for the organization. Stepping aside also can open up room for others to advance through the corporate structure and bring new ideas and creativity to the organization.

2. Outgoing leaders should consider taking on some major or even controversial projects before his or her successor takes over. This allows a fresh beginning and a smoother transition.

3. In professional service firms, a democratic process should be established for selecting successors. This can be a nominating committee of some sort, or a group that helps identify what is needed in the next leader.

4. Suggested steps toward an effective succession planning process include:
   - Develop criteria for filling key positions.
   - Assess individual candidates against these criteria.
   - Create individualized leadership development plans for internal candidates.
   - Identify gaps that may need to be filled by external hires.
   - Conduct ongoing reviews of the timing of anticipated key position openings.
   - Facilitate an annual talent management review process.

"If you look at succession more in terms of 'next steps,' it's much more positive. A lot of the projects I'm working on now I wouldn't have had time for if I were still Managing Partner."

—Bill Hermann

"Bill's basic message was, 'This is your time. My time is past. Feel free to come to me for advice, but I'm not going to be looking over your shoulder.' "

—Gordon Krater

The Next Chapter

By Bill Hermann, Managing Partner Emeritus

We're back where we started—the moment of succession from one leader to the next. The day we elected Gordon Krater as our new Managing Partner signaled not just a new era for Gordon and for Plante Moran, but also for me. In my new role as the firm's leader for service industry businesses, I have worked to reinvent my role, and also to reinforce a long tradition at the firm of former Managing Partners staying out of their successors' way.

My decision to remain involved also helps send the message that stepping down does not necessarily mean stepping out.

How the vacating CEO or Managing Partner leaves the stage, and what he or she does thereafter, is an important step in a smooth post-succession transition. Both the former and the new leaders are facing new territory. Some solid plans for both individuals helps the transition for all.

The adjustment for the departing leader can be significant. I still remember a phrase by the Managing Partner I succeeded years ago. He strode into my office and said, "The king is dead; long live the king." I asked him what in the world that meant. He said it meant that while it was great being king, it was quite a big adjustment not being king.

And he was right. One of the first things former leaders deal with are questions from all kinds of constituents that range from nosey to downright insensitive: "What did you do wrong?" "Were you booted?" "Are you retired?" "What are you going to do?" "Why are you sticking around?"

No amount of messaging will change this. The former leader simply needs to move into whatever direction he or she has chosen. One alternative is to remain in a productive role at the firm, as I have chosen to do. However, the way this is done can hurt or help transition.

First, it helps to be physically removed from the "C suite." An office on the other side of the building or a different location altogether can help reinforce to the firm a new leader indeed is in place. I moved into our Ann Arbor office, located some 40 miles away from our home offices in Southfield, Michigan.

Second, as described in this book, former leaders should offer advice only when approached. Certainly, some initial words of guidance can be appropriate. After all, there will be no one else the new leader can identify with regarding the overwhelming new responsibilities and challenges he or she faces. Frankly, as I look back to when I assumed the role of Managing Partner, it was clear I had no clue what I was getting into.

So I spent a lot of time with Gordon and other Managing Partner candidates. I told them some of the highs and lows and disappointments they will feel. I told them how people may react when things don't go their way.

A healthy understanding of human nature will go a long way. We have an awful lot of incredibly competitive people. And trying to keep them in a position where everyone is a winner is quite a juggling act.

Most people may think they want to be a boss for the money or prestige. They may overlook the reality that it's a tough job, and many people who haven't been there don't understand that.

This is a key message: It really, really *is* lonely at the top. It's lonely because when you are Managing Partner, there will likely be fewer than two people who have been there before and are still around in semi-retirement or full retirement. While these people can be enormous assets, their limited number, and the fact that they may have been in charge in an era that has long passed—and these days, that's about five years—render their support crucial but limited.

When you lead and make decisions that affect a lot of people, you, and only you, make the call. And you accept the credit or take the blame. If this is something you can't fathom, consider another career path.

New leaders need to understand they cannot go it alone. So assembling a team of senior managers as advisors—not unlike the president's cabinet—is a crucial form of support. Selecting this team should take into consideration not just credentials and experience, but the expertise of each member. They should be chosen to help "fill in the gaps." That's one of my favorite phrases. Everyone, including CEOs, have certain strengths and areas where they need support. Identifying your "gaps" and then choosing a team to help offset them makes a lot of sense.

Most important in any selection of your team is trust. You have to identify who you can trust, and then you have to trust them. And if things go wrong, remember: It was your decision.

Gordon and I both learned as Managing Partners that a management team's regular observations, feedback, and suggestions help keep us vital and open to new ideas. You have to be adaptable, and you can't be too tied in. You can't have that bachelor's syndrome of living by yourself and getting mired in your own perspective and ways of doing things.

Keeping an ear out for ideas from all staff has its value, as well. The average age of your staff is likely to be much younger than you are, so you had better be listening. By always being willing to watch and listen, you help guarantee your own success, all the while providing that seamless transition to the next leader. The combination of your actions—and your firm's culture and processes—can all but guarantee a sustainable future for your organization.

As Bill and Gordon gathered thoughts and ideas for this book, they compiled some lists of basic advice for leaders.

From Bill Hermann:

- Find teachable moments—in groups and in private.
- Don't let anyone out-prepare you.
- Stretch your imagination whenever possible.
- Don't let anyone else take the blame.
- Give away as much credit as possible.
- Give honest and immediate feedback.
- Don't hold grudges.
- Allow people to make mistakes; just make sure you have their back.
- Always have alternatives.
- Give someone you don't like a try.
- Be willing to disagree and accept others' ideas; just make them better if necessary.
- Hold people accountable.
- Ask lots of questions.
- Observe potential successors under pressure—making decisions, leading teams—and as colleagues.
- Be compassionate.
- Protect your and the team's family lives.
- Take vacations.
- Encourage everyone else to take vacations.

From Gordon Krater:

- Do great work.
- Constantly remind yourself that clients pay the bill.
- Remember all the people around you who help you serve your clients.
- People are attracted to an optimist. Be positive.
- Leave people better than you found them.
- Treat everyone—from CEO to your boss's assistant—well.
- Give others plenty of credit.
- Hold people accountable.
- Praise your people often.
- Follow the Golden Rule.
- Never burn bridges.
- Include others who think differently than you do.
- Lead by example.
- Don't ask others to do what you won't do.
- Embrace technology and change.
- Provide solutions, not problems.
- Build your career in a way that is sustainable.
- Always do the right thing.
- Have fun.

Commitment Statement

In this Appendix, we offer some examples of Plante Moran's foundational documents:

Our Commitment

For the counsel and guidance of present and future members of the Plante Moran team, we set forth this brief statement of what Plante Moran is, our Philosophy, and the relationship between our Philosophy and our firm's Spirit, Vision, and Strategy. Our ongoing attention to these matters will continue to be among the most important responsibilities of each of us.

Our Mission

Plante Moran will be a broad-based professional certified public accounting and consulting firm. We will proactively pursue and respond to the needs of clients by rendering a wide range of high-quality, professional business consulting services commensurate with our collective abilities and representing true value in relation to cost. Although we will continue to operate the firm in conformance with sound business practices, we will remain a professional firm with our primary emphasis on serving, not profit.

Our Philosophy

Plante Moran is guided by our Philosophy that is based on certain core values and perhaps best expressed in condensed form by the Golden Rule: "Do Unto Others As You Would Have Others Do Unto You." It is symbolized by the Plante Moran gold ruler and implied in the Plante Moran motto: "We Care." We care about our clients, we care about our work, we care about our families and our communities, and we care about each other.

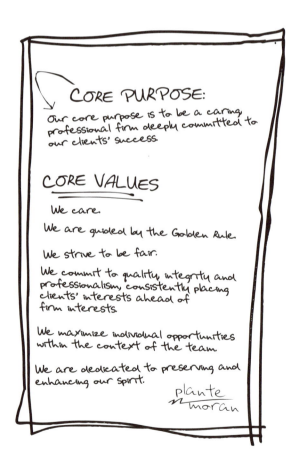

Although the Plante Moran Philosophy can be summarized by the Golden Rule, it is comprised of many principles, such as those in our Statement of Principles, namely: Service, Ethics, Recruitment, Compensation, Individual Progress, Advancement, Teamwork, Delegation, Education, Leadership, Individual Freedom, Communication, Decision Making, the Common Good, and Balance.

These important principles include fairness; doing everything reasonable for the individual up to the point of harming the team; helping the individual to become all that he or she is capable of becoming; optimizing, rather than maximizing, our financial success; and doing what is right for the right reasons, with major emphasis on the long-range consequences of our decisions.

Although we will continue to expand and refine the Principles embodied in the Plante Moran Philosophy, our emphasis will be on communicating, exemplifying, and living the Golden Rule day in and day out.

Our Spirit
Our Plante Moran Spirit is the sum of our attitudes and feelings toward clients, each other, ourselves, the firm, its Principles, and its Philosophy and how we collectively and individually practice the Golden Rule. We are committed to maintaining and enhancing our Spirit by constant attention to our Philosophy, by reinforcement through adding only persons of goodwill, by individually practicing and supporting behavior that exemplifies caring attitudes, and by discouraging behavior that does not.

Our Vision
Little of consequence is accomplished unless there is first a dream. After each dream comes the work to make the dream come true. Our Vision is that we will be relentless in our pursuit of:
- Providing 100 percent of our clients with unmatched service, and
- Having 100 percent of our staff members realize professional and personal fulfillment while taking joy in making the dream come true.

Statement of Principles

- Because we recognize that a professional accounting and audit organization cannot long exist on what it once was or now is, but only on what it aspires to be, and
- Because we recognize that, to a large extent, the future of Plante Moran will depend upon the aspirations of its staff members,
- We are setting forth a Statement of Principles for the counsel and guidance of present and future members of the firm.

Principle of Service

- It is our intent to serve the needs of our clients by providing professional services of the highest quality. We will continue to develop our capabilities and processes to anticipate and satisfy client needs, always placing their interests ahead of our own. At the same time, we will help each client to become as self-reliant as practical.

Principle of Ethics

- It is our intent to be guided by the highest level of ethics consistent with the Golden Rule. Individual staff members will not be required to perform work that offends their personal principles.

Principle of Recruitment

- It is our intent to recruit those individuals, regardless of race, color, creed, gender, religion, age, national origin, or handicap, who have the attitudes and capacities for service, learning, and growth.

Principle of Compensation

- It is our intent to compensate staff members as fairly as possible, based on their contribution and the success of the firm. Staff members should realize that there is a direct relationship between their compensation and the value of services they are rendering. Therefore, to a large degree, individual staff members are responsible for their own earning level. Learning and improving will result in enhancing one's earning potential.

Principle of Individual Progress

- It is our intent to encourage each staff member to progress within the firm at his or her own pace, subject to the overall welfare of the firm.

Principle of Advancement

- It is our intent at all times to turn first to our own staff members when contemplating promotions or filling higher-level staff openings. Recruitment of staff from outside the firm will be undertaken only when it appears to be in the best interest of our clients and the firm as a whole.

Principle of Teamwork

- It is our intent to work as a team to serve our clients. We will always attempt to utilize the best skills and capabilities available to satisfy client needs.

Principle of Delegation

- It is our intent to assign staff members to the level of work that will enable them to utilize their highest abilities over the greatest portion of their working day. This requires that the work be delegated to the experience level at which it can be performed most effectively.

Principle of Continuing Professional Education

- It is our intent to undertake or utilize those staff training programs, seminars, and work experience that, in our best judgment, will contribute most to the professional growth and advancement of the individual staff members and the firm. It is also our intent to provide ready access to information related to continued staff development.

Principle of Leadership

- It is our intent to encourage and develop our staff members to be leaders within the firm and our communities.

Principle of Decision-Making

- It is our intent to maintain a timely yet thorough decision-making process, with decisions made at the most appropriate level. We will strive to be effective by keeping a balance between participation and efficiency.

Principle of Individual Freedom

- It is our intent to create an atmosphere that maximizes individual freedom with as few rules as possible. While this freedom requires greater individual responsibility, we believe this kind of environment maximizes the opportunity for each of us to flourish professionally.

Principle of Communication

- It is our intent to maintain a free flow of meaningful information to and among staff members, and to encourage staff members to contribute their ideas and suggestions regarding business and policy matters. In this way, we hope to retain many of the advantages that come from being a small, close-knit group, even as we grow in number.

Principle of Common Good

- It is our intent that the firm shall not be operated for the personal advantage of any one member or group, but for the common benefit of all staff members.

Principle of Balance

- It is our intent to provide an atmosphere where balance is sought and celebrated: balance between work and family, between work and play, between professional accomplishments and personal pursuits, between head and heart, and between individual freedom and the good of the team. Inherent in this is the understanding that balance varies for each staff member and is a lifelong, constantly changing challenge.

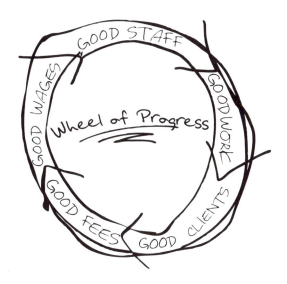

Wheel of Progress

- The Wheel of Progress was developed by our founding fathers and is an icon that we use frequently. Nothing depicts the business case for having a strong culture more clearly than the Wheel of Progress. It recognizes the linkages between a strong culture, focus on people, and the inevitable outcome: good client service.

Diversity

- Plante Moran recognizes there are multiple attributes of diversity—including but not limited to age, gender, race, geography, marital status, and religion—that are so valuable to our firm and our clients. An inclusive mindset recognizes that diversity creates strong, creative businesses that attract the best and brightest talent and are better positioned to proactively address the changing work environment.

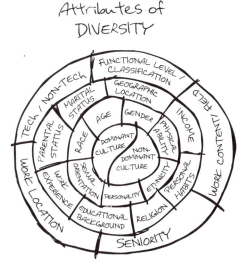

Source: Implementing Diversity, Marilyn Loden, McGraw Hill Books, Burr Ridge, IL, 1996. By permission.

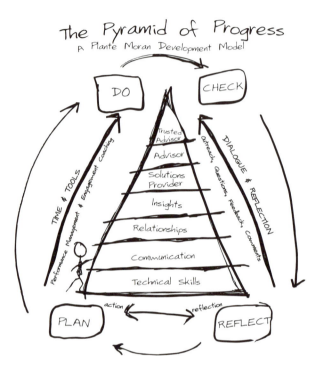

The Pyramid of Progress
A Plante Moran Development Model

Pyramid of Progress

- Our Pyramid of Progress is a foundational model designed to help staff understand the process of developing their skills as professionals in serving clients, building practices, and growing and developing each other. It measures staff progression up through the pyramid, and helps them set the right goals to build upon existing relationships and competencies and develop new ones.

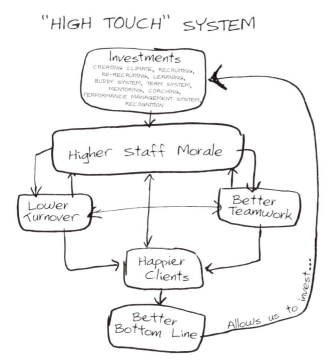

"HIGH TOUCH" SYSTEM

Investments
CREATING CLIMATE, RECRUITING,
RE-RECRUITING, LEARNING,
BUDDY SYSTEM, TEAM SYSTEM,
MENTORING, COACHING,
PERFORMANCE MANAGEMENT SYSTEM,
RECOGNITION

Higher Staff Morale

Lower Turnover

Better Teamwork

Happier Clients

Better Bottom Line

Allows us to invest...

"High Touch" System

- We believe that culture is not processes and procedures, but you don't build a strong and successful CPA firm without processes and procedures. Investing in staffing systems and processes improves the bottom line. Our high touch system is designed to promote retention and prevent turnover—and create better client service. Low turnover saves dollars and leads to high morale and high retention. The ability to retain high-quality staff leads to better teamwork, better future leadership, and a more diverse firm. The result is great client service, an excellent reputation, and better financial results.

((✫))

Sources

Chapter One

"Corporate Culture & Performance," John P. Kotter and James L. Heskett, iLead, www.ilead.com.au/ideas/strategic_thinking/organize_culture.html.

"One-Firm Firm" concept: http://davidmaister.com/articles/1/101/.

Chapter Three

The Triarchic Mind: A New Theory of Human Intelligence, Robert J. Sternberg, http://education.stateuniversity.com/pages/2104/Intelligence-TRIARCHIC-THEORY-INTELLIGENCE.html.

"Millennials in the Workplace: R U Ready?" by Knowledge@W.P. Carey, http://knowledge.wpcarey.asu.edu/article.cfm?articleid=1580.

U.S. Department of Commerce.

U.S. Small Business Administration Office of Advocacy, U.S. Census Bureau, Corp. for Enterprise Development, http://www.score.org/minority_stats.html.

Implementing Diversity, Marilyn Loden, McGraw Hill Books, Burr Ridge, IL, 1996

Aberdeen Group.

National Women's Business Council.

Sources

Chapter Four

"Pacer Theory" William N. Dember, *The Psychology of Perception,* New York: Holt, Rinehart & Winston, 1960.

Chapter Five

Coaching and Mentoring, Richard Luecke, Harvard Business School Publishing Corp., Boston, Mass., 2004.

Marilynne Miles Gray, Mentoring Solutions Inc., 2005.

The Art of Managing Professional Services, Insights From the Leaders of the World's Top Firms, Maureen Broderick, Prentice Hall, Upper Saddle River, N.J., 2010.

Chapter Six

"Succession Planning: How Everyone Does It Wrong," Stephen A. Miles, Forbes.com, July 2009.

Index